LITTLE KNOWN ENGLAND

MARKET DRAYTON, SHROPSHIRE
WITH THE RIVER TERN

LITTLE KNOWN ENGLAND

Rambles in the Welsh Borderland
The Cotswolds, The Chalk Hills
and the Eastern Counties

By

Harold Donaldson Eberlein

CLASSIC EDITIONS

This edition digitally re-mastered and
published by JM Classic Editions © 2007
Original text © Harold Donaldson Eberlein 1930

ISBN 978-1-905217-79-3

FOREWORD

LITTLE KNOWN ENGLAND as a title will probably challenge the criticism of more than one class of readers. Some will say that no part of England is little known, at least little known to an extent that would justify the title. Others will say that more territory ought to have been included under this heading. To the latter can only be pleaded the exigencies of space, along with an expression of hope that portions of the country now omitted may be dealt with on some future occasion.

As an actual fact, there are many parts of England that are very little known by the majority of native-born Britons who could go there at almost any time and so never go at all. In the same way summer travellers from beyond the Atlantic, who come back to the old homeland either to see what manner of place their forebears went from to hew out new abodes in the Western world, or else, perchance, to refresh on the spot their memory of our common history, are often at a loss to find reliable information to guide them anywhere beyond the most obvious places of interest.

The time at the disposal of these summer visitors is usually all too brief, and too commonly they aim at rapid, "comprehensive" tours enabling them to see a few of the most noted places. All the rest they leave untouched, to their own great loss. By such whirlwind expeditions England can never be really seen nor known. There is neither time nor opportunity to perceive the soft beauties of the countryside or to grasp the quiet charm of the villages and market towns with their endless wealth of association. And all of these go to make up a great part of the real England.

The tide of touring sweeps past much that is most beguiling and leaves the traveller unsuspecting and blind to numberless allurements. Through the chances of modern touring, the greater part of Shropshire and Herefordshire, along with much of Gloucestershire, Oxfordshire, Berks and Bucks, both the Briton off for a sight-seeing holiday and the traveller from beyond England's shores leave untouched, while most of East Anglia, except the seaboard resorts, is a *terra incognita* save to those who live there.

The present volume, therefore, will confine itself to this little known area, which, curiously enough, forms approximately a U-shaped strip across the face of the country. This affords a decided difference and contrast—three Eastern counties parallel—two on the Western border, with a connecting link of counties which again form a microcosm of variety in themselves. It will leave out those places more or less touched by the customary tide of travel, and dwell on the seldom visited but not less engaging parts whose rewards can be fathomed only as their intimacy is cultivated. And these sure rewards are to be found in the striking contrasts and manifold diversities of the countryside, in the people and their ways, in their local customs and history, and in the visible evidences of that history enshrined in the varied and characteristic buildings.

I have to thank Professor A. E. Housman for his very kind permission to include verses from " Wenlock Edge " in "A Shropshire Lad," published by The Richards Press, which appear on page 12; and Mr. John Masefield for the stanzas from "London Town," from The Collected Works published by Messrs. Heinemann.

Thanks are also due to the following for their kind permission to reproduce the drawings and photographs with which this work is illustrated: Dr. G. Granville Buckley, plates VIII$_2$ and XXII$_2$; Brian C. Cook, Fig. 2 and the maps;

T. Raffles Davison, Fig. 20; Sidney Newcomb, Fig. 28; W. Curtis Green, A.R.A., plate xix_1 and Fig. 24; Sydney R. Jones, Figs. 4, 8, 10, 11, 12, 14, 17, 18, 21, 22, 25; His Majesty's Stationery Office, from Royal Commission on Historical Monuments: Essex, Central and South West, $xxxv_1$; A. H. Mottram, Fig. 23; Roland W. Paul, F.S.A., Fig. 15; The Rev. F. Sumner, plate $xliv_2$; Victoria and Albert Museum, $xxiii_2$, xxxiv, xxxix, $xlvii_2$; F. R. Yerbury, $xxxii_2$; Brian C. Clayton, of Ross-on-Wye, Herefordshire, v, vii_1, x_1, xi_1 and $_3$, xii, xiv_2, xl_2, $xlii_2$, $xliii_1$, $xliv_1$; Cyclists' Touring Club Gazette, "from Drawing by C. Patterson," Fig. 19; Herbert Felton, F.R.P.S., vi_1, $xiii_1$, $xviii_1$, $xxxv_2$; Frith & Co., Reigate, x_2, xiv_1, $xxii_1$, $xxix_2$, $xxxiii_1$, $xxxvi_2$, xli_1; *The Leominster Journal*, ix_2; Will F. Taylor, i, iii_1, $xvii_2$, xxv_2, $xxxi_1$, $xxxiii_2$, $xxxviii_2$, $xliii_2$, $xlvii_1$; J. Valentine & Sons, Dundee, ii_2, iv_1, $xxvi_1$, xl_1; Robert Scott, from Timmin's "Nooks and Corners of Shropshire," Figs. 3 and 7, and Timmin's "Nooks and Corners of Herefordshire," Fig. 9. The others are from the collections of the author and publishers, many by Horace Dan and the late W. G. Davie.

In closing, the writer can wish nothing better than that those who read these pages may eventually learn to know and love those parts of "Little Known England" here described as does he for whom they hold a treasure of long and pleasant memories.

HAROLD DONALDSON EBERLEIN.

London,
   May 1930.

CONTENTS

Page

FOREWORD v

Chapter

I THE WELSH BORDERLAND: SHROPSHIRE AND
   HEREFORDSHIRE

   Bridgenorth—Morville—Much Wenlock—Wenlock Edge—
   Stretton Dale—Corve Dale—The Clees—Clee St. Margaret
   —Ludlow—Cleobury—Bromfield—Leintwardine—Bramp-
   ton Bryan—Clun—Stokesay—Acton Burnell—Langley—
   Shrewsbury — Wigmore — Pembridge — Kilpeck — The
   Golden Valley—Abbey Dore—Ledbury—Goodrich Castle .   1

II THE ROLLING UPLANDS: A PASSING GLANCE AT
   THE COTSWOLDS IN GLOUCESTERSHIRE AND
   OXFORDSHIRE

   Cheltenham—Owlpen—Bibury—Burford—Bourton-on-the-
   Water—The Swells and Slaughters—Stow-on-the-Wold—
   Chipping Campden—Bourton-on-the-Hill 53

III THE CHALK HILLS: THE BERKSHIRE DOWNS AND
    THE BUCKINGHAMSHIRE WOODED CHILTERNS

    Dorchester—Abingdon—Uffington—Down Tracks—New-
    bury—The Hendreds and Hagbournes—Steventon—Ewelme
    —Fingest — West Wycombe — Jordans — William Penn—
    Chalfont St. Giles — Langley — Penn Village — Chenies —
    Bradenham—Aldbury—Ivinghoe 65

IV THE EASTERN COUNTIES: NORFOLK, SUFFOLK
   AND ESSEX

   General Features—Quiet scenery—Hempstead—The Rodings—The Pant Valley—Finchingfield—Pargetting—The
   Dunmows and the Flitch—Thaxted—Saffron Walden—Clare

CONTENTS

Chapter   Page

—Hawkeden—Hartest—Bury St. Edmunds—Knettishall
Church — Wymondham — Hingham — Swaffham — King's
Lynn—East Dereham—Wells-next-the-Sea—Cley—Knapton
—Southwold—Lavenham—Kersey—Stoke-by-Nayland—
Castle Hedingham   87

V OUTLINE SUMMARY OF THE FOUR DISTRICTS
     AND MAP SECTION

Practical Touring Hints—Shropshire—Herefordshire—The
Cotswolds—The Chalk Hills—The Eastern Counties: Essex,
Suffolk, Norfolk—A FEW PRACTICAL TOURING HINTS . 114

INDEX TO TEXT AND ILLUSTRATIONS   .   .   . 129

MAPS

The Welsh Border South of Shrewsbury
The Cotswolds
The Berkshire Downs
North Bucks and The Chilterns
East Anglia and Essex

Interior, Blakeney Church, Norfolk.

LITTLE KNOWN ENGLAND

CHAPTER I

THE WELSH BORDERLAND

Shropshire and Herefordshire

Bridgenorth—Morville—Much Wenlock—Wenlock Edge—Stretton Dale—Corve Dale—The Clees—Clee St. Margaret—Ludlow—Cleobury—Bromfield—Leintwardine—Brampton Bryan—Clun—Stokesay—Acton Burnell—Langley—Shrewsbury—Wigmore—Pembridge—Kilpeck—The Golden Valley—Abbey Dore—Ledbury—Goodrich Castle.

LONDON, of course, is the least known part of all England. London, like Rome, is inexhaustible, and no one can ever hope to know all of it. If you care to seek, you can find within London's bounds everything from pre-British, British and Roman remains down to the latest gramophone records or the newest feminine bagatelles from Paris, to say nothing of all else under the sun, fetched hither from the farthest corners of the earth. As Rome once was, so London has become the heart of the world, and is likely so to continue from her geographical position alone, if for no other reason. And of other reasons there be many.

But, however much we may love, marvel at and feel the homely spell of the dear old grubby, splendid city on the Thames, whatever curious rewards we may reap by prying into her infinitely varied past or her complex present, a perpetual half-consciousness of her amazing, manifold medley of antiquity and modernity haunts the mind. Crowding memories of myriad actors in her mingled tragedy and comedy sometimes force themselves upon us with crushing weight. Now and again the wraiths of Tyburn's felons seem to rise up from the scene of their punishment, point ghostly fingers at the thousands bowling past them along Bayswater, and bid the folk of to-day take

I

flight to the country where unspoiled nature banishes the oppression born of composite humanity's too thronging recollections.

So, then, let us heed the warning and leave the task of delving into the little-known curiosities of Mother London's past for some other occasion. Let us betake ourselves straightway from the heart of things to the banks and hills of southern Shropshire, whose out-of-the-way charms are known *about*, but very little known and tasted. If we cannot chant sincerely with Masefield,

" And London Town of all towns I'm glad to leave behind,"

we can sing with him most whole-heartedly,

" Then hey for croft and hop-yard, and hill and field and pond,
With Bredon Hill before me, and Malvern Hill beyond,
The hawthorn white i' the hedgerow, and all the spring attire
In the comely land of Teme and Lugg, and Clent, and Clee, and
    Wyre."

   .   .   .   .   .   .

" Then hey for covert and woodland, and ash and elm and oak,
Tewkesbury inns, and Malvern roofs, and Worcester chimney
    smoke,
The apple trees in the orchard, the cattle in the byre,
And all the land from Ludlow town to Bredon church's spire."

   .   .   .   .   .   .

" So hey for the road, the west road, by mill and forge and fold,
Scent of fern and song of the lark by brook, and field, and wold,
To the comely folk at the hearth-stone and the talk beside the
    fire,
In the hearty land, where I was bred, my land of heart's desire."

With the joyous lilt of Masefield's verses ringing in our ears, we take the road through Ombersley, that precious village of " black and white " half-timbered houses that welcomes the traveller with an inn to match—one of the most typical of England's old hostelries—as you come from Worcester. Whether, like Masefield, you claim this " land of heart's desire " through long familiarity, or whether you are seeing it for the first time, you cannot be insensible to its perennial charm. Perennial charm it surely has ; each season of the year brings its own rewards. Spring, with the hawthorn abloom and the orchards laden with billowy clouds of blossoms ; autumn, with gorgeous foliage and the hedges crimsoning with haws ; summer, with its lush greenery in field and wood, and flocks of sheep dotting the pasture lands ; winter, in dull browns and greens or glaucous with the frost, clumps of vivid mistletoe nested in the orchard boughs, blue smoke curling into the crisp air from cottage and farmhouse chimneys, and the labourers at their hivernal tasks looking for all the world mediæval enough to be the originals for the woodcut illustrations of *Piers Plowman*—such incidents of the way never fail to make the journey a genuine delight.

Past Ombersley the country soon begins to roll again, and after Kidderminster, with its busy hum and manufacture, it is not long before we plunge into the tumultuous contours of southern Shropshire. The main roads are steep enough in places and many of the ascents are long, though not of such a nature as to cause trouble ; but if the motorist turns aside into the deep lanes and by-ways he will find many a grade on the " banks " sharper and more trying to his car than any the writer has met on the roads over Alps or Apennines. Such country is bound to have no end of diverting nooks, and wise is he who accepts Shropshire's bidding to drop down or climb up her less travelled by-roads. Only don't do it in a big car ; better go in a little car with a strong engine or, better still, in the saddle or a-foot. As William Cobbett remarked a hundred years ago " those that travel on turnpike roads know nothing of England."

Going on towards Bridgenorth, the vale of Severn is on our left with water meadows, long reaches of water, and deep combes furrowing the high ground beyond. On our right, the oak-clad hills rise steeply above, making you feel that Shropshire is a land enclosed and isolate from the counties to the east. Quatford and Quatt we pass. The former is a tiny, peaceful hamlet so well concealed by great oaks and the deep cutting in the red sandstone through which the main highway drops abruptly downhill, that you can easily go by without being aware of its presence. Tidy, bucolic, placid, it no wise suggests the winter of discontent

3

an invading band of Danes spent here more than a thousand years ago. The name of Danesford hard by is the only reminder of this episode : the Danes, indeed, left very little impression on Shropshire.

Quatt is almost on the borders of the Low Town at Bridgenorth, and we turn into the long street that runs to the bridge almost before we know it. Old half-timbered houses, spick and span with fresh buff paint or whitewash, are crowded in between demurer Georgian dwellings of brick on both sides of the way. Some of these orderly Georgian exteriors, however, enclose much older structures, for it was the custom all through England in the eighteenth century to make earlier-built houses conform to the current mode by giving them a new brick outer dress. The owners were keen, above all things, to be in the fashion. Hence it is that many a town or village street wears a complete Georgian masque hiding structures that may really date anywhere from the fifteenth century to the seventeenth. Bridgenorth, fortunately, has kept a good many of its half-timber buildings without change, despite eighteenth century architectural emulation and later additions.

As you cross the stone arched bridge to the base of the rocky hill on which the High Town stands, the view up the Severn Gorge, especially in the spring, creates one of those clear-cut cameo pictures that lodges ever after in the memory. But the bridge is not long. At its farther end the road turns sharp to the left and toils up a precipitous winding ascent that brings you to the High Street on the upper level.

Perched aloft on top of its red cliffs, Bridgenorth is blessed with a most dramatic site. It is hard to say whether it is best to see it first on a sunny spring morning, wrapped in a haze of young foliage, or to come upon it at night, with the Severn shimmering below and twinkling lights dotted over the hill and along the terraces, just like an Italian hill town in the dark. There is certainly some compensation in getting to such a place on a cold, rainy night, catching the cheer of its lights glittering in the wet, pushing up the long climb in the comforting assurance that you are reaching your goal, and then sitting down to a hot rum toddy on a high-backed oak settle beside the fire in a half-timbered inn,

4

a good dinner in prospect with a grilled steak, and sound port to follow.

Whether you arrive by day or by night, it is always a treat to turn into the bottom of Bridgenorth's High Street, old houses of varied ages at each side and, directly ahead, the half-timbered Town Hall standing in the middle of the thoroughfare on its open arcade of red sandstone. Perhaps it is market day and, if you have a fancy that way, you can go up into the coffee-room of The Swan—very like the cabin of an eighteenth century ship it is—and look down upon one of the still unspoiled characteristic sights of English rural life.

The winding climb around the nose of Castle Hill is a comparatively modern improvement. Before it was made, the main artery between the High Town and the Low Town was the old Cartway, a series of such steep pitches that you wonder how wheeled vehicles ever got up or down. It is bad enough to follow it a-foot in either direction. The short-cut links between the High Town and the Low Town for pedestrians are the " steps " or passages, too narrow to be called streets. The Stoneway Steps and Saint Mary's Steps (Plate II) are the chief of these, but there are also the Cannon Steps, Saint Leonard's Steps, the Granary Steps, and various others. All these " steps " are, as their name implies, nothing but flights of steps broken by occasional steep ramps, and lined on each side by houses and garden walls. They are the only means of approach to the terraced dwellings which grow out of the rock on such a diversity of levels that it is easy to see how the old saying arose that Bridgenorth folk could walk along and look down their neighbours' chimneys to see what they were having for dinner.

A touch of modernism in the shape of a steep funicular railway, running obliquely up the cliff from the Low Town to the High Town, lends comfort nowadays to the lazy and the feeble who have occasion to go either up or down. This mechanical convenience seems incongruous when you learn that this very same rock harbours a number of cliff dwellers whose forebears, at a time to which " the memory of man runneth not back," burrowed far enough into the sandstone

5

to make themselves comfortable if not altogether com-
modious abodes (Plate II).

Of Bridgenorth prior to the seventeenth century, but little
remains, thanks to the disastrous fire that almost completely
destroyed the town in 1646. Saint Leonard's church, noted
for its exceptionally wide nave, escaped total destruction but
has endured sundry episodes of restoration. The half-
timbered town hall, built between 1650 and 1652 to replace
its ruined predecessor, preserves its outward aspect but
within has suffered from the over-zealous efforts of nineteenth century "restorers." Near Saint Leonard's church
is the little half-timbered house where dwelt Richard Baxter
about 1640, before his succession to the cure of Kidderminster. Out of "his unfeigned love to them, who were
the first to whom he was sent to publish the Gospel," he
dedicated one of the editions of his *Saints' Everlasting Rest* to
the people of Bridgenorth. The *Saints' Rest* most of us
know merely as a name in connexion with seventeenth
century literature. Few ever open its pages or note the
effect it had in its day. Whether we approve the author's
theology or politics, our own generation might do worse
than dip into it now and then as a stimulus to good English.

Bridgenorth's other literary shrine, which also escaped
the fire, is the black and white house near the bottom of
the Cartway where Bishop Percy was born in 1729. Built
in 1580, the birthplace of the learned bishop who compiled
the *Reliques of Antient English Poetry* is now the Boy Scouts'
headquarters. Though not altogether enveloped in the
atmosphere of archæological minstrelsy, the building is
well maintained and not defaced in a manner that has
befallen too many buildings that deserve reverent preservation.

As to the old Norman castle, built in 1101 by Robert de
Belesme, Earl of Shrewsbury, there is nothing left but a
leaning block of masonry, part of the ancient keep. For
this wholesale destruction we may thank the Lord Protector.
Fortunately the ruin has been made the excuse for creating
a pleasant park. Besieged by the Roundheads in 1645, in
March 1646 the castle was subjected to a three weeks'
bombardment from Pampudding Hill, the traditional site

6

of the castle built in 943 by King Alfred's daughter, Queen Ethelfleda, as a defence against the Danes. The bombardment failing to produce any effect, the Parliamentarians set to work to mine the rock. Then, to save his men, Sir Robert Howard, the Governour of the Castle, capitulated in April, and he and his garrison were allowed to march out with the honours of war. Three months later, the Cromwellians blew up the castle.

Despite all the battering, destruction and "restoration" suffered at one time or another, Bridgenorth has managed to keep its characteristic flavour. But, having enticed the visitor thither, it is better to leave him to explore for himself the "walks" and terraces girdling the rock and to make his own discoveries.

Fig. 1.—Old House at Whitchurch, Shropshire.

Drawn by E. A. Ould.

Shropshire is approximately a rectangle in shape with Shrewsbury, the county town, just about the middle. And Shrewsbury marks the boundary between the tumbled, hilly southern part and the quiet, pastoral north. The

7

north, with its placid meres, its farm and pasture lands, and its tidy old towns like Newport, Market Drayton (Plate I, Frontispiece), Whitchurch (Fig. I), and Wem, is a pleasant enough country, but our present concern lies not there. Our quest is in the hilly south with its " banks " and " hopes," its wooded heights and well-watered valleys, its deep lanes, narrow by-ways and villages whither few strangers ever penetrate; westward towards the Welsh border with its ruined castles (Plate III); and thence southward into Herefordshire.

Leaving Bridgenorth behind, we traverse a rolling, winding hedge-bordered road, now and again passing through stretches of rich woodland. Every turn discloses fresh vistas of shady dells or swelling hillsides, gracious even in their sombre winter browns and glorious at other seasons, whether clothed in the soft sheen of early spring, the full-bodied greenery of summer, or the glowing hues of autumn. The Shropshire hedges, and those of Herefordshire, have an individual quality distinguishing them from most hedges elsewhere. Whether raised on hedge-banks or set on the level of the fields, they are broader and thicker at the bottom than the usual hedges in other counties and their close-clipped tops have a more rounded contour. Oftentimes holly is mingled with the thorn, and not seldom do you see holly trees at regular intervals growing directly out of the hedge, for all the world like some garden enclosures depicted in Renaissance Italian mural paintings.

> " Blest is the eye 'twixt Severn and Wye,
> But thrice blessed he 'twixt Severn and Clee ! "

Whence came these lines, it would be hard to say; but their truth is more and more forcibly driven home the better you know the countryside; no bit more warrants the praise than that immediately hereabouts. As you drop down the hill to Morville village and start the opposite ascent, across the fields to the left is the grey little Norman church that in 1118 replaced an earlier structure of the days of Edward the Confessor. Higher up the hill, and nearer the road, is the hall, erstwhile the priory. Amongst the changes since the suppression of the Monasteries, is the addition of a whimsical

8

PLATE II.

ST. MARY'S STEPS, BRIDGENORTH

ROCK HOUSE, THE HERMITAGE, BRIDGENORTH

PLATE III.

WHITTINGTON CASTLE, SHROPSHIRE

A VIEW FROM WENLOCK EDGE

though delightful seventeenth century front; its austerity is not the least part of its appeal.

A few more ups and downs, and then a sharp drop brings us to Much Wenlock, lying in a bowl of the hills, though itself at no little elevation; its site is one of those upland vales or " hopes " frequent in this part of Shropshire. Some old inns and a number of good timbered houses are scattered about the town; one of them may have sheltered King Charles after the Battle of Worcester. Wenlock's chief gems are its half-timber Guild Hall, "buildid over ye Prisonne," and the ruins of its once splendid Priory.

Fig. 2.—Perigrinating Stocks, Much Wenlock.

Drawn by Brian C. Cook.

Supported on stout oak columns above the open market, the upper storey of the Guild Hall has two large rooms with open-timbered roof and mullioned casement windows leaded with small lozenge panes. Above the Judge's Bench in the room set apart for the Court of Assize are carved the Royal Arms of Queen Elizabeth and along the roof timbers of the adjoining Council Chamber runs the admonitory legend IUDICIUM VERUM IUDICATE: ET MISERICORDIAM FACITE. Both rooms are oak-panelled and the rich carved ornament is of fine quality.

" Ye Prisonne " over which the Guild Hall is " buildid "

9

is nothing more pretentious than a small village cage or lock-up; most of the open ground-floor space is kept for the market. A far more efficacious engine of correction, still kept at the Guild Hall, is a pair of peregrinating stocks (Fig. 2), curiously equipped with small spool-like wheels and a long iron handle to draw it about. Persistent drunkards used to be set in this punitive " pram " and given a ride while the townspeople pelted them with addled eggs and vegetables past their maturity.

Hard by the Guild Hall is the ancient church of Saint Milburga, Much Wenlock's royal patron saint, daughter of Merwald and granddaughter of Penda, Kings of Mercia. Just around the corner from the church—which, by the way, has a number of features worth seeing—we turn into the Bull Ring and go on past a ruined bit of the gatehouse that once gave entrance to the Priory precincts.

The original nunnery, once presided over by Saint Milburga, fell a prey to the fury of the Danes. In the time of Edward the Confessor, Earl Leofric, husband of the Lady Godiva, re-established the ruined foundation but it fell again to decay and remained of little account till Roger de Montgomery, about 1071, refounded the community as a Priory of Benedictine monks attached to the French Abbey of Cluny. In the reign of Richard II its foreign dependence ceased and at the Dissolution it was one of the richest and most important monastic establishments in England.

Earl Roger began the buildings, parts of which may still be seen amongst the ruins, but the greater portion of the fabric, as it stood at the Dissolution, was Early English. Of Earl Roger's Norman work, the most striking remnant is the beautiful chapter-house with its interlaced arcading and chevron mouldings, unsurpassed as English Norman ornament. The cloister garth is now a garden carpeted with luxurious turf and bounded by clumps of clipped yew; between their sombre masses bright flowers liven the setting. In the centre of the greensward is the carved stone lavabo, wrought with Scriptural subjects, where the monks used to wash—not altogether unlike an old Italian well-head and evidently of glorious design before its mutilation.

Beyond the chapter-house and the fragment of cloister

arcade, a great part of the Prior's Lodging (Fig. 3) remains intact and in perfect preservation. All its mediæval domestic arrangements are still clearly visible, though adapted to modern needs. When the monasteries were dismantled and destroyed, the whole of the Prior's Lodging at Much Wenlock was fortunately spared, but a demon in the shape of a nineteenth-century house agent demolished part of it. His iniquitous hands were stayed—Heaven be praised!—before he could complete his fell purpose, and the remnant well deserves the pride and care bestowed by

Fig. 3.——Chapter House Ruins, and Prior's Lodgings,
Much Wenlock Abbey.

Drawn by H. T. Timmins.

its occupants, who have also taken proper measures to prevent further disintegration of the Priory Church ruins.

One road out of Wenlock leads to Broseley, associated with clay pipes, pottery and the " Broseley dragon " pattern made famous by Caughley china. But a short distance along this way, the tiny village of Barrow perched on its rise arrests us by its diverting little church with unmistakable bits of Saxon work in both chancel and tower. Somehow, though, caprice drags us back from the road towards Broseley and the Severn, which we left behind at Bridgenorth, and impels us toward the north-west where, just up a gentle rise on the farther borders of Wenlock, the road forks and forces us to make a decision between two equally beguiling alternatives. To the right the Shrewsbury road beckons us down Wenlock Hill, one of the hilliest main roads in the kingdom, with a gradient of 1 in 6 at steepest, unfolding a really fine view as you drop down into the vale with the Wrekin heaving up his broad shoulders ahead to the right. To the left the road goes climbing on up and runs for miles along the very top of Wenlock Edge.

Wenlock Edge is a great hilly ridge running from south-west to north-east, its south-eastern side rising from Corve Dale by tumbled, rolling slopes to its long undulating crest, like a vast sea wave ; its north-western side—again like a wave, just about to break—is a precipitous drop into Ape Dale, with the land billowing up again on the farther side till the swelling contours culminate in the heights of Ragleth Hill, Caer Caradoc and the other lofty sentinels of the range that forms one wall of the narrow Stretton valley.

Wenlock Edge (Plate III) is a place of many moods and ever changing lights. At all seasons it stirs a yearning sense of pride in anyone through whose veins there runs a single drop of Shropshire blood.

Away to the right, at a bend of the distant Severn, little Wroxeter nestles on the spot where once stood the strong Roman city of Uriconium whose ruins are still there. Perhaps you look from the Edge on a bleak, windy November day. Unbidden come to mind those lines from Professor A. E. Housman's *Shropshire Lad* :

> " On Wenlock Edge the wood's in trouble ;
> His forest fleece the Wrekin heaves ;
> The gale, it plies the saplings double,
> And thick on Severn snow the leaves.
>
> 'Twould blow like this through holt and hanger
> When Uricon the city stood :
> 'Tis the old wind in the old anger,
> But then it threshed another wood.
>
> .   .   .   .
>
> To-day the Roman and his trouble
> Are ashes under Uricon."

Briton, Roman, Saxon, Norman—how we see them cross the stage and vanish! And, at long last in the pageant, troop Parliamentarians and Cavaliers. Mid-way the Edge, on its southern slope, stands the grim old sixteenth-century pile of Wilderhope (Fig. 4) in a remote wilderness, difficult of approach in any but the best of weather. Here lived Major Smallman, a staunch Royalist. One day a troop of Cromwellians surrounded the house, intending to capture the Major. Smallman dashed up the turret staircase, jumped from an upper window, fled to the stables and,

Fig. 4.—" Wilderhope," Shropshire.

Drawn by Sydney R. Jones.

mounting his horse, galloped towards the crest of the Edge, his would-be captors in hot pursuit and gaining on him. Reaching a flat rock at the verge of the precipice, he put his horse over the edge. The horse was killed but Smallman's fall was broken by the branches of a crab-tree and he made his way home again in safety after his pursuers had given up the chase.

Half way along Wenlock Edge, and not far from Wilderhope, a steep main road drops down into Ape Dale, passes by Hope Bowdler and, through a cleft in the Caradoc range, brings you to Church Stretton. The Long Mynd, breaking on the view as you come through this rift in the Caradoc hills, is a sight that sinks indelibly into the memory. Be it in autumn, when the upper slopes are motley with emerald green and dry bracken the colour of the red deer, or be it in the season when gorse and heather weave a royal mantle of purple and gold, nothing could be more truly regal than the bold form and bulking mass of this western barrier to Stretton Dale.

The front of the Long Mynd (Plate iv) (note that the *y* in Salop place names is spoken short *i*), towards Stretton Dale is seamed by the fast streams into deep and winding combes, such as the Carding Mill Valley, or the Ashes Valley; one cleft contains the cascade known as the Light Spout. Beyond their steep slopes of heather and bracken is the main ridge, which reaches at the Pole a height of 1,636 feet, about the same as Caradoc across the Dale. From this spot is a typical glorious prospect of Border hills, valleys, woods, hamlets and churches, with a glimpse of the County town, and the blue plain of Shropshire's northern half. All is silent moorland around except for a lonely keeper's cottage, one of the highest dwellings in the west country, or indeed all England. An old green track threads the gently undulating ridge; it was referred to in mediæval documents as " The King's Highway on Long-munde," and in summer carries quite a fair amount of traffic, with even a few hardy motor cycles.

But in winter, especially under snow, the expanse of combe and slope and ravine is difficult, even dangerous, to traverse, and the last fair in November at Church Stretton had the cheerful name of " Deadman's Fair,"* from the mishaps that attended farmers trying to make their way to upland holdings across the hills. The Rev. Donald Carr, a former Vicar of Winstanstow, has left a record of his wanderings for three nights and two days in the snow when returning across the Long Mynd from taking an afternoon service in winter at Ratlinghope.†

* Referred to in Professor A. E. Housman's Last Poems, 1922, practically a second series of *A Shropshire Lad.*
† *A Night in the Snow*, by the Rev. Donald Carr (*circa* 1862).

Church Stretton's inclination to become a holiday haunt has encouraged some regrettable episodes of modernisation and obscured somewhat the town's ancient character, but All Stretton, farther up the dale towards Shrewsbury, and Little Stretton, farther down towards Ludlow, have preserved their earlier aspect. Three parallel roads run through the dale—the old Roman road or Watling Street, the modern highway, and the railway—for Stretton Dale has always been a main artery of traffic since early British times, and long before for aught we know.

Watling Street, though now but little used through most of its length and in some places virtually abandoned, tempts you to forsake the main highway and go exploring.

Leaving the Strettons behind, by the time you near the southern end of Stretton Dale the impulse to strike off from the beaten line is irresistible. You turn aside into one of the little by-ways where there are few finger-posts, to tell you where you are bound. Not one half the endless good things in the less-known parts of little-known England will you find till you resolutely push into out-of-the-way corners.

Just before Ape Dale and Corve Dale draw close together, near the southern end of Wenlock Edge, there are several by-roads that wind among the lower hills and " banks " and bring you out into Corve Dale. You will probably go through Diddlebury or Delbury (have it which way you like), before crossing the dale and plunging into the tumultuous country that billows upward in woodland and downs into the bold mass of the Clee Hills, those old volcanic heights which, with the Wrekin to the north and the Long Mynd to the west, dominate the whole of southern and central Shropshire. Delbury church or Diddlebury church—whichever you elect to call it—is a delightful architectural jumble embodying Saxon work with portions in nearly every ecclesiastical mode that has obtained in England since.

From Delbury it is but a short distance through the apple orchards of the dale to Munslow whose scattered cottages are dotted about in a thoroughly irrelevant manner. If night is at hand, Munslow is a good place to put up, for it boasts a fairly comfortable inn, and such are none too plentiful in the dale. At the roadside pubs accommodation would be difficult, although the landlords are a kindly lot and would willingly do all they could to make you comfortable at a pinch. If the day is young, however, impatience to get into the hills again prods you on through Tugford. The old church, dating partly from Norman times, the mill and the stream—a tributary of the Corve— all combine to form a picture that bids you linger, but by this time the urge of the hills is full upon you and up you must go.

Which road you take from the Dale to attain the Heath depends on your mode of locomotion. If you are walking or in the saddle, you can take the short road; if you are driving a car, especially if it be a large one, you had better take the longer way around which is quite stiff enough. The Heath is really on a western buttress of Brown Clee Hill and at no mean elevation. The Chapel on the Heath (Plate IV) is one of the most perfect examples of a small Norman church to be found in England. Fortunately, nothing has ever been done to it by later generations to spoil its architectural integrity. There, for over eight hundred years, service has been held Sunday after Sunday, except sometimes in bitter winter when—so the story goes— if the parson found only " two or three gathered together," he and they would adjourn to a neighbouring farmhouse kitchen and matins would be said beside a roaring fire.

If the Chapel on the Heath inspires you with a keen sense of antiquity, you will get an even more vivid thrill from the durability of human effort if you continue your climb up to the fortified Roman camp at Nordy Bank, which is in a remarkably good state of preservation. From Nordy Bank you had better go a-foot if you wish to reach the summit of Brown Clee Hill, but whatever puffing and sweating you endure clambering up the steep, rock-strewn bank, to the northern summit, Abdon Burf, will be more than justified by the view you get. You can look down on every other hill in Shropshire, and over a wonderful panorama, for you will find no greater elevation nearer than the mountains of Wales. To the north the Wrekin's rounded dome rises isolated in front of the plain called Vale Royal. Near at hand to the south Titterstone Clee thrusts up his conical crest in rivalry. To the west and north-west Wenlock Edge, Caer Caradoc, Ragleth, the Long Mynd, the Stiperstones and Long Mountain make a goodly band of companions; beyond them rise the mountains of Wales. To the south-west the High Vinnall lifts its once shaggy barrier beyond Ludlow town; far away to the south-east the jagged edge of the Malverns cuts the sky and far, again, beyond the Malverns the Cotswolds shew their line. Truly a fair sight, and worth a man's effort to gain !

The twin Clees are really the erupted cores of old volcanoes, and the basaltic granite of which they are composed, known as " Dhu stone," is too hard to be carved, but it makes the finest road material in the world. On Titterstone the granite has overlaid workable coal seams, the highest in Britain, and the slopes are dotted with high-lying hamlets. The schoolhouse of the village of Clee Hill is 1,100 feet above sea level.

Instead of climbing the western face of the Brown Clee— of necessity a footslogging job—it is equally remunerative to make the circuit of the hill, especially as the quarrying operations have lately spread on to the western face.

Not far from The Heath is the little hamlet of Abdon, which gives its name to the northern summit of the Brown Clee. From its modern church rambling lanes rise to the flank of the great hill just at the 1,000 feet level, with a western view of sweeping hill ranges far into Wales, about as fine from the highest point itself. The road turns round the northern edge of the hill, high above the spire of Ditton Priors, the terminus of a light railway from Cleobury Mortimer. Only a few wire transporter lines give evidence of the presence of industrialism, but the view is utterly transformed—the border hill peaks and ridges are replaced by the mighty expanse of the Midland plain, stretching to Wolverhampton in the blue distance. The road now threads its way along the opposite or eastern face of the Clee, winding in and out of the hill combes, always at a height of about 1,000 feet. It is a most delightful drive among ornamental plantations, laid out by a former Lord

Boyne of Burwarton in honour of his bride. Finally you are deposited between the Clees on the main Ludlow Bridgenorth road near its 1,200 foot summit. It is an exhilarating dash down back to Ludlow, unless you'd rather go on !

Almost from the Chapel on the Heath, you will find a wooded road that drops rapidly downhill and, turning sharply at the bottom, brings you suddenly into the village of Clee Saint Margaret's, an idyllic secluded spot that seems to belong to some old romantic tale. The rose-bowered cottages, set in a fold of the hills, the very forms of the trees, all make you feel that it is something lifted bodily from another world and that you are privileged to see it only by grace of some potent enchantment. Having got in, the only apparent road out you are told goes over a steep ridge and is practically hopeless. Upon enquiry you discover that your road out is *in* the brook, and through the brook you go for nearly an eighth of a mile, a footpath running beside the babbling road. Then Clee Brook goes on about its business to join the Corve, the road comes on dry land again, and you plunge into deep lanes bound for Hopton Cangeford—Hopton-in-the-Hole, it used to be called.

To have your sole occupancy of the road interrupted in one of these narrow, deep lanes may be embarrassing or may merely occasion some absurd incident. Once I dropped a friend at Hopton Cangeford Vicarage for the night and then went on into Ludlow by deep lanes and gated roads over " banks " and through dells. Next morning when I went back for him, a big white-faced Herefordshire cow had picked out the deep lane as a choice place to graze and I had to drive her ahead of the car for nearly a quarter of a mile, tootling vigorously to keep her moving at all—she had a very phlegmatic disposition. When I turned down the side lane to Hopton my friend was driving two pigs and four geese up ahead of him. It took the combined ingenuity of us both to find a spot wide enough to effect a passage and then induce the barnyard creatures to stop there long enough to let us get by.

The saffron crocus grows hereabouts and, in autumn, its lavender-coloured blossoms often make a brave show in the fields. William Cobbett greatly admired the purple crocus in an orchard at Bollitree, Herefordshire, in September, 1825. The farmers, however, loathe it. The daughter of a Vicar of Hopton Cangeford, weary of the usual vegetable garnishings, once decked the church for the harvest-home service with saffron crocuses. Several of the neighbouring farmers looking into the church on Saturday afternoon and seeing the mauve decoration straightway protested to the Rector that they couldn't come and praise the Almighty in a church adorned with nasty poisonous weeds, so out went the crocuses and in came cabbages, turnips and carrots in their stead.

Of all the roads into Ludlow town, none is so beautiful, none has such truly dramatic quality as the road from Hereford. It drops down a sharp rise at the end of Bringewood Chase and, just as it rounds a bend, there is Ludford Bridge, a splendid mediæval stone-arched structure over the Teme. Opposite is the town, piled up on an eminence, its west and south sides washed by the Teme whose waters murmur over the weirs. The bridge continues the downward slope of the road to the farther bank; thence a broad street sweeps straight uphill to the ancient south gate. Within the gate (Plate v) this goodly street goes right up to the brow of the hill in the centre of the town. The sudden view of this broad steep roadway bursting upon you unexpectedly, after the narrowness of the gateway, makes you catch your breath.

Many of the houses on both sides shew stately Georgian fronts; others, of earlier date, proclaim the local half-timber tradition. It is as noble an entrance as any town in England can boast.

That observant old traveller, John Leland, wrote:

"The town of Ludlow is very propre, welle walled and gated, and standeth every way eminent from a Botom. In the side of the Town, as a Peace of the Enclosing of the Walle, is a fair Castel. (Plate v). Within the Town, even yn the mydle, is one Paroch chyrch. There be in the Wall 5 gates. Broad gate leadeth to Broad Street, the fayrest part of the Towne. The Castel standeth on a strong Rocke, well ditched, between Corne gate and Mille gate. The Paroch church is very fayre and large, and richly adorned, and taken for the fayrest in all those Quarters."

The comeliness of Ludlow, that so favourably impressed Leland in the time of Henry VIII, strikes us with the same force. The Castle, then in full repair and inhabited by the Lords President of the Council of the Welsh Marches, is now a ruin. The town has grown and many new houses have arisen since Leland wrote his *Itinerary*. But the essential spirit of the place has remained unchanged. The poise, the spacious dignity and the subtle engaging quality that Leland felt and recorded, Ludlow still possesses.

The houses built since Leland's time are nearly all of them worthily fashioned in the modes of succeeding centuries; some of the older buildings are the same his eyes beheld. It would be hard to find anywhere else more or better half-timber examples in the typical Shropshire and Herefordshire manner; their overhanging storeys, carved bargeboards, and moulded or carved corbels, go far towards preserving the old aspect of the streets.

The " Paroch chyrch " of Saint Lawrence, " very fayre and large, and richly adorned " is, of course, one of the most significant features of the picture. Its tall red sandstone central tower dominates the whole of Ludlow. It utters the town's voice, so to speak, by its pealing bells on Sundays, market days and other occasions of public note. A truly splendid Perpendicular pile with a lofty open lantern, formed at the crossing by the central stages of the tower, the church has almost the port of a cathedral. Fortunately the fabric suffered comparatively little damage either at the Reformation or during the Commonwealth, so that the interior is still rich in ancient glass and carved woodwork.

The approach to the church affords a dramatic contrast; from the bustle of the high street and the market square, a narrow passage called the " Scallens " cuts between the shops and brings you by a sudden transition into the quiet of the churchyard. When the mayor, in his robes of office and preceded by his mace-bearer, comes through the " Scallens " and enters the church porch to attend service, the picture is complete. At the east end of the churchyard is the old half-timbered and carved " Reader's House," (Fig. 5), a well preserved sixteenth century structure.

PLATE IV.

ENTRANCE TO THE ASHES VALLEY, ON THE LONG MYND

THE HEATH CHAPEL, ABOVE CORVE DALE

PLATE V.

THE NARROW GATEWAY, BROAD STREET, LUDLOW

LUDLOW CASTLE FROM WHITCLIFF, ABOVE DINHAM BRIDGE

Beside it a narrow passage goes down a flight of steps directly into the posting yard of The Bull whose fifteenth century row attests the age of the hostelry, which the stranger might not suspect from the orderly Georgian front turned towards the street.

Not the least factor in the charm of Ludlow is the unspoiled old hostelries, of which three deserve especial mention— The Feathers, The Angel and The Bull. The Bull, like so many old inns throughout England, was refronted late in the eighteenth century and, when it put on its Georgian mask to the outer world, it also underwent some interior "modernising." There are, or were, however, in the dining-room those "armes in colours, sitch as fewe can shewe" that once adorned the ancient round chapel of the Castle. At The Feathers, across the street, the public rooms have preserved all their pargework decoration and carved panelling; the street front, too, is completely unspoiled and is one of the best examples of "black and white" work in all Shropshire. Not far off, after passing through the Bull Ring and turning into Broad Street at the Butter Cross to take the road to Hereford, at the end of

Fig. 5.—The Reader's House, Ludlow.

Drawn by E. Hodkinson.

Butcher Row you will find The Angel. The Angel is a curiously engaging composite of features dating from the seventeenth century to the nineteenth.

Ludlow Castle is splendid from any point of view; even in its ruinous state it gives a vivid idea of what must have been its majesty when it was kept in full repair. Muse in retrospect upon a company who played their parts in England's making. There was Roger de Lacy, Lord of the Manor of Ludlow when Domesday Book was compiled; he it was who built the Castle. Joce de Dinan, who was lord in Stephen's troublous reign, waged ceaseless feud with his neighbour, Hugh de Mortimer of Wigmore; having captured the doughty Hugh by a ruse, Joce de Dinan shut him up in one of the loftiest towers which still bears the name of Mortimer of Wigmore. Few of us ever think of this as we go through Mortimer and Wigmore streets in London.

By a deed of the last year of Stephen's reign, it appears that Hugh de Lacy then laid claim to lands in Herefordshire then held by Joce de Dinan, and it is likely that these conflicting claims caused the hostilities between Hugh de Lacy and Joce de Dinan anent which the following romance is told. Incidentally, it explains how Ludlow Castle passed to the family of Fitz Warine. Fulke Fitz Warine, who eventually came into possession of Ludlow Castle, was heir to the Castle and Honour of Whittington, through his mother, Melette, daughter of William Peverel.

When Fulke was seven years old, according to the custom of the time, he was placed as a page in the family of Joce de Dinan to learn the practice of knightly exercises. As he grew up he became "handsome, strong, and of goodly stature." At the time of the fiercest quarrels between Joce de Dinan and Walter de Lacey, Fulke had reached the age of eighteen. One summer's morning Joce de Dinan espied an armed host on Whitcliff under the banner of his mortal enemy, Sir Walter de Lacy. He thereupon ordered part of his knights to arm and mount speedily to defend Ludford Bridge. Soon afterward went Joce with five hundred knights and men at arms; crossing the water, they utterly routed the invaders. Walter de Lacy, seeing his standard lost and his men scattered, fled along a road near the banks of the Teme towards Bromfield.

Joce, seeing de Lacy in flight, pursued him unattended and overtook him in a little valley within sight of the castle. Already wounded, de Lacy was on the point of being made prisoner when three of his knights suddenly appeared and came to his aid. This encounter Joce's lady with her two daughters, Sibille and Hawyse, saw from a tower of the castle. Terrified at the danger threatening Joce, who was now alone against four, they rent the air with their screams. Fulke, who had been left behind because of his youth, rushed to learn what was the matter and asked Hawyse the cause of their alarm.

" Hold thy tongue," she replied, " thou resemblest little thy father who is so bold and strong ; and thou art but a coward, and ever will be. Seest thou not where my father, who has cherished and bred thee with so much care, is in danger of his life for want of help ? And thou art not ashamed to go up and down without paying any attention ! "

Stung by this reproof, Fulke hastened to the hall of the castle where he found an old rusty helmet. This he put on as best he could, for he had not yet reached the age of bearing armour. Seizing a great Danish axe, he ran through the stable which was close to the postern leading to the river. Joce de Dinan, overpowered by numbers, was already unhorsed and beaten to the ground. Fulke, arriving at this moment, with his great axe clove the back-bone of one of Lacy's men who was binding the fallen Lord of Ludlow. With a second blow he split the skull of another of de Lacy's men.

Joce was soon remounted and Walter de Lacy with his remaining companion, Arnold de Lisle, who was already badly wounded, were easily made prisoners. They were brought to Ludlow Castle and confined in the tower called Pendover. They were kindly treated and the ladies of the household often visited them. Amongst these ladies was " a very gentle damsel," Marian de la Bruere (Marian of the Heath), who was smitten by the courtly mien of Arnold de Lisle and allowed herself to be seduced by his fair words and promises of marriage. Having thus put herself in his power by her imprudence, she was further induced to help the prisoners escape from a window by a rope of towels and napkins tied together. Walter de Lacy then sent to his father in Ireland for soldiers, determined to avenge himself on Joce de Dinan. After a short period of hostilities,

23

the two barons were reconciled by the good offices of their neighbours.

Soon after peace was thus restored, Fulke Fitz Warine was wedded with great ceremony to Hawyse de Dinan. After the festivities were ended, Joce de Dinan with his household and his son-in-law, and Warine the father of Fulke, went to " Hertland," leaving Ludlow Castle to the care of thirty trusty knights and seventy good soldiers, " for fear of the Lacy and other people."

Directly Joce de Dinan had quitted the castle, Marian de la Bruere, who had stayed behind on pretence of illness, sent a message to her lover, Arnold de Lisle, telling him the state of the castle and praying him to come to her. She promised to let him in through the same window by which he and de Lacy had escaped. Arnold told de Lacy this and got his consent to making an attempt on the castle. Providing himself with a leather ladder, according to Marian's directions, one dark night he took with him a thousand knights and soldiers, most of whom he concealed in the woods on Whitcliff. The rest he ambushed in the gardens beneath the castle walls.

When Arnold, with a soldier carrying the ladder, came under the tower window, his mistress was waiting and threw down a cord, pulled the ladder up and fastened it. He mounted it and Marian took him to her chamber. The ladder was left hanging from the window. Meantime, the soldier who had carried the ladder went back to the gardens and brought the ambushed soldiers. An hundred armed men climbed the ladder into the tower of Peverel, made their way to the inner ward, and slew in their beds the knights and soldiers left to guard the castle. Then they issued from the castle, opened the Dinham gate to let in the rest of Lacy's men and, stationing soldiers at the end of each street, they burnt the town and massacred the inhabitants, sparing neither woman nor child. At daybreak, Marian, who was in bed with her lover, was wakened by the shouts of the victors. Looking from the window, she discovered the treason enacted during the night. In an agony of despair she seized Arnold's sword and thrust it through his body; then she threw herself out of the

24

window and "broke her neck." When Walter de Lacy
got word of the successful attack, he came with all his men
and took possession of Ludlow Castle.

It was through the marriage of Fulke Fitz Warine with
Hawyse de Dinan that the Fitz Warines later came to hold
Ludlow.

John Lackland once seized the Castle in the wars with
his barons; here Henry III concluded a treaty of peace
with the Welsh prince Llewellyn. Hither Edward IV sent
his two boys for safe keeping—those hapless lads afterwards
murdered in the Tower of London; and here Prince
Arthur sojourned for a time, during his nominal honey-
moon. But of all the vanished company, perhaps it is
pleasantest to think of Sir Henry Sidney, Lord President of
the Council of the Welsh Marches, who lived here in Queen
Elizabeth's reign, and in the last quarter of the sixteenth
century built within the Castle precincts the lodgings whose
ruins are still there to remind us of that gentle and brilliant
family who lent lustre to a splendid age. It was at this
time, one summer's day, that the Sidney children disappeared; long and anxious search failed to discover them,
and the whole countryside was alarmed. At last they were
found in a secluded combe, called Sunny Gutter, in Bringewood Chase across the Teme. This incident later inspired
Milton to write the Masque of Comus, and the masque,
appropriately enough, was first performed in Ludlow
Castle. During the Civil Wars, Ludlow Castle was held
for the King and it was the last stronghold in Shropshire
to fall into the hands of the Parliamentarians. In 1689 the
Council of the Marches was abolished; after that date the
Castle was allowed to fall to rack and ruin until, in the
present day, the decay was stayed and the precincts made
into a town park.

No sight could be fairer than what you see from Ludford
Bridge. For all the " pretty chapel . . . of Saint Catherine "
is gone, " there be three fayre arches in this bridge over
Teme " and the ancient structure itself is always good to
look upon from any quarter. But you must stand upon it
to appreciate it to the full and gaze upon the river winding
over the weirs at your feet, Whitcliff's rugged wall beyond

and, still beyond again, the wide sweep of the hills with the dark growth of Bringewood Chase. On the other side of the bridge, there's the river widening out in quiet pools with the steep wooded bank rising up behind Ludford Village ; its ancient church, its hospital for aged pensioners, its timbered houses half-buried in greenery, and its gracious manor house—all these bring pleasure too poignant to express.

No sight could be fairer than the outlook from Whitcliff over Ludlow Town of a peaceful Sunday eventide, when the shadows lengthen and the daws circle upward from the churchyard yews as the bells begin to peal.

Old Churchyard was right when he wrote :

" The town doth stand most part upon a hill,
    Built well and fayre, with streates both long and wide ;
The houses such, where straungers lodge at will,
    As long as there the counsell lists abide.
Both fine and cleane the streates are all throughout,
    With condits cleere and wholesome water springs ;
And who that lists to walk the Towne about
    Shall find therein some rare and pleasant things ;
But chiefly there the ayre so sweete you have
    As in no place ye can no better crave."

May God save Ludlow long, and keep it as it is—and damn suburbia that already clutches at its north-eastern flank !

If you would really get into the spirit of southern Shropshire and absorb some of its charm, make Ludlow your headquarters for the time and ramble thence in different directions : north, east and west—south will take you into Herefordshire, whither we come later.

Take the eastern road from Ludlow town and it will lead you up over the southern slopes of Clee Hill and bring you on, over magnificent rising and broken ground to Cleobury Mortimer, a town of unusual historical associations outshining its material estate. Of Cleobury Mortimer Leland says : " The village of Clebyri standythe in the Rootes by est of Cle Hills, seven myles from Ludlow, in the way to Beaudeley." (It is actually eleven and all most hilly.) In the Middle Ages it was part of the great Honour of Mortimer, hence the name; its castle was destroyed during the Barons Wars. But the tie with the house of Mortimer yields place to another mediaeval claim to interest : William Langland, he who wrote the *Visions of Piers Plowman*, was born in Cleobury in the fourteenth century, so that Shropshire, and especially this part of it, gave the background for the work of the Lollard Poet. In the High Street of Cleobury is a time-worn block of red sandstone on which, tradition says, they laid the body of Prince Arthur who died while travelling over this road from Ludlow to Bewdley. They bore him on to Bewdley, and thence on to Worcester for burial in the Cathedral.

Cleobury has yet another association with a well-known historical personage. Its lord was once Queen Elizabeth's " sweet Robin," Robert Dudley, Earl of Leicester, of whom it was said, " He was a compleat Gentleman in all suitable employments ; an exact seaman, an excellent architect, mathematician, physician, chymist and what not. He was an handsome, personable man, tall of stature, red haired, and of admirable comport ; and above all noted for riding the great horse for tilting, and for his being the first of all that taught a dog to sit in order to catch partridges." No wonder the wilful Queen was strongly attracted towards this fascinating figure.

The north-east road from Ludlow takes you up to 1,200 feet over the high saddle between the peaks of Brown Clee and Titterstone Clee and brings you to Bridgenorth, through Burwarton and Cleobury North. Not far off, and near the course of the Rea as it comes down from Brown Clee, are some sequestered little villages and townlets that have retained their primitive air. Old Leland says : " Cle Hills be holy in Shropshire. The highest Parte of Cle Hills is cawlyd Tyderstone. In it is a fayre playne grene, and a fountaine in it. There is another Hill a 3 Miles distant from it cawlyd Brown Cle." Leland was wrong. Brown Clee is a little higher than his more southerly twin—it took accurate instruments to prove this, so no shame to Leland, for they are both noble hills. The " fayre playne grene " and the fountain

27

have yielded their place to coal pits and the quarries whence they get the volcanic granite " Dhu stone." Along the Bridgenorth road over the saddle between the Clees, the tumbled, broken contours of the land are gashed abruptly by precipitous glens with a never-ending play of lights and shadows.

A more northerly course from Ludlow soon brings you to the " Old Field," where Corve Dale broadens out before the Corve pours its waters into the Teme on their way to join the Severn at Worcester. " Old Field," dotted with " tumps," tumuli and bunkers, and accented with clumps of gorse between, is one of the few level stretches of ground anywhere near the town, being used both as a race course and golf links. Possibly some of the barrows above the bones of ancient chieftains do duty as bunkers.

From the " Old Field " it is but a trifling distance to Stanton Lacy, a fascinatingly picturesque village at the end of the " Rootes " of Titterstone Clee. Stanton Lacy church contains a great deal of admirable Saxon work—" long and short " masonry and the characteristic wavy courses, to say nothing of an excellent round-arched doorway. It is, indeed, one of the best specimens of pre-Norman building in England. The story goes that Saint Milburga—King Penda's daughter whose traces we have already found at Much Wenlock—built the original church as a thank-offering for safe riddance from the ardour of a too persistent suitor, a Welsh prince. In answer to her prayers, a sudden flood swept down the Corve and blocked the pursuing lover's further progress toward the princess-saint, who had already gained the farther bank.

About equally distant from the other side of the " Old Field " is the pleasant village of Bromfield whose ancient stone bridge over the Onny is guarded by the " Twelve Apostles " (Plate vi). The " Twelve Apostles " are reduced to *nine* towering poplars that serve as a distinguishing landmark from all the way across Corve Dale. According to Domesday Book, Bromfield was a place of some consequence even in the Conqueror's day, There was an important priory of Benedictine monks here at a not much later date, and the wealth and size of the foundation are attested by the Priory Gatehouse and a few ruins and remains of other conventual buildings.

From Bromfield by hilly lanes you can go to the village of Downton on the Rock, skirting the fine park of Downton Castle, the property of the Arkwrights. At Downton there is a blatant modern church complete with stone spire. The old church, unroofed and ruinous, has been decaying rapidly for the past years and little now remains of the typical wooden Tympanum which spanned its chancel above the rood loft. Just by Downton the River Teme has cut its way through a deep limestone gorge at the Hay Mill, and you have only to cross a field by a cart track from the lane to the cottage and disused mill. The public is admitted on Tuesdays to the splendid walks which thread the steep leafy ravine, though possibly access may be obtained to the fine view by the start of the gorge at the mill bridge by polite strangers at other times.

From Bromfield you can also take the Leintwardine-Wales road over a hill ridge and near Mocktree Common at an elevation of eight hundred feet. Here, by the way, you come into the most northerly point of Herefordshire and continue in what is a sort of promontory of that county thrust upward into the southern boundary of Shropshire until you have passed through Leintwardine and turned northward again from Brampton Bryan. After turning the Fiddler's Elbow—a well-named stretch of road that seems to consist mainly of very acute angles made necessary by the strange contour of the hill—you have a sharp drop down towards Leintwardine. Below you on your left is a deep combe with a dense hanging wood over the tops of whose trees now and again you see the valley of the Teme far beneath.

In Roman Britain, Leintwardine was the station of Bravinium ; the fosse and vallum of the Roman fortifications may still be traced. Roman stations were not established through whim, and the justification for Bravinium was the meeting of natural highways and the confluence of the River Clun with the Teme. Incidentally, the trout and grayling inhabiting these waters lure thither the disciples of Izaak Walton.

At Brampton Bryan, a few miles farther on, there are the ruins of one of the old border castles which William the Conqueror granted to the Mortimers, from whom it subsequently came to Sir Bryan de Brampton. Eventually the castle came by marriage into the Harley family, one of the very few border families to side with the Parliament in the Civil Wars. During the absence of Sir Robert Harley, his wife, Lady Brilliana Harley, withstood a five weeks' siege by the Royalist forces under Sir William Vavasour and Colonel Lingen ; the siege was raised when tidings came of the King's defeat at Gloucester, but the castle was invested again the following spring and ultimately taken and dismantled. Hard by Brampton Bryan is Coxwall Knoll, where Caradoc is said to have made his last stand against the Romans. Coxwall Knoll is a rugged, isolated hill that affords a striking incident in the splendid hill setting of this village at the outskirts of the Forests of Radnor and Clun, serene enough now but filled with memories of a stormy past. Its one annual excitement is a horse and pony fair that has been held since time immemorial. Luxuriant yew hedges and yew trees are peculiarly characteristic of all this region, but the great yew hedge surrounding the Hall—which has succeeded the castle as a dwelling place and separating it from the church—is a thing worth seeing.

Turning northward from Brampton Bryan, the first village is Bucknell (Plate vi), where the cross-road from the church runs along in the river, with a raised footpath and handrail at the side, very much like the road out of Clee St. Margaret. The rest of the village is in keeping with the primitive and picturesque quality of the watery roadway. The name of the little river, the Redlake, they ascribe to its running red with blood after Caradoc's last fight with the Romans. From Bucknell the road bears gradually north-eastward across the vale to the River Clun, leaving the ruins of Hopton Castle on the left. Hopton was once a mighty Norman fortress and continued a formidable stronghold till 1644 when the Parliamentarians " slighted " it after they had put its loyal garrison to the sword and sent the Governour off to gaol.

If you follow the course of the Clun, it will bring you to Clungunford, Aston-on-Clun, Clunbury, Clunton and, finally, to Clun itself. According to the old couplet :

"Clunton and Clunbury, Clungunford and Clun
Are the sleepiest places under the sun."

Before making for Stokesay Castle and then pushing on for Stretton Dale, Acton Burnell and Shrewsbury, it is worth while to turn aside at Aston-on-Clun and make a detour to Clun itself.

In spite of its grim grey stone houses that look as though they might have been fetched from across the Welsh border, Clun out of all the Clun galaxy of townlets is by far the fullest of interest, for it has a splendid old church, the ruins of the Castle, the Hospital of the Holy and Undivided Trinity, and the Buffalo Inn, once part of the Clive property, with a name reminiscent of Lord Clive's attempt to domesticate the Indian buffalo in England. Clun Castle is sometimes supposed to be the original of the Garde Doloreuse in *The Betrothed*, though the description does not fully accord, and tradition has it that Sir Walter Scott wrote the first three chapters of the novel in the Blue Room of The Buffalo. Whether this be actually true or not, Clun Castle, or rather what is left of it, is well worth seeing. It was one of the strong borderland fortresses built by the Normans to hold the turbulent Welsh in check, and protect the people of the border counties from their raids. The Fitz Alans were the lords of Clun, and their fief, which became a semi-independent barony, was called the Honour of Clun. Amongst other rights appertaining to the Lord of Clun was the power of capital punishment and there is record of one of his vassals holding a messuage and croft by the curious tenure of delivering at Shrewsbury the heads of felons to certify that the proper persons had been executed. Time and again during the Middle Ages Clun Castle was stormed and sadly battered. Leland wrote that it was "sumewhat ruinus" in his day, "though it hath bene bothe stronge and well builded." As a finishing touch to its long story as a fortress, the Roundheads dismantled it when they got possession in the Civil Wars.

It eventually passed to the Dukes of Norfolk who derive from it their second title of Baron Clun.

The River Clun sweeps in a great bow around the base of the castle hill and, not far away, the old hump-backed stone bridge with bold sparlings and five unequal arches crosses the stream. On the far side a sharp ascent leads to the church dating from Norman times, massively built, with a great square west tower. Just above the line of the nave roof the tower stops abruptly and is capped by a squat stone-tiled roof of pyramidal shape broken mid-way by a louvre stage. The lych-gate is an exceptionally fine piece of oak timbering ; amidst the yews of the churchyard the tombstones nearly all bear Welsh names.

The one other relief from the grim little houses of the town is the Hospital of the Holy and Undivided Trinity at its eastern border, a refuge for decayed tradesmen, founded by the Earl of Northampton in 1614. Built about a well turfed courtyard, the structure itself is full of architectural charm, but still more engaging are the old pensioners themselves, each of whom receives every year on Founder's Day " a gown ready made of strong cloth or kersey, of a sad colour, to wear upon Week Days ; and also every fourth year, upon Trinity Sunday," has " delivered unto him to wear, such a livery gown of blue cloth lined with bayes, with the Founder's cognisance set on the sleeve, to wear upon Sundays and Festival Days." Nether garments and shoon, too, needless to say, are provided by the Founder's endowment, so that the pensioners are fully clad, and they have due allowance for food and other maintenance.

The exigencies of continuing the rambles caused the author to retrace his steps from Clun, but the cyclist, pedestrian, or even the adventurous motorist need not adopt so tame an alternative. If the latter is equipped with a small car, easily manoeuvred, with excellent brakes, and is not afraid of stiff ups and downs, he can enjoy the delights of some first-class hill-climbing, by taking the northern road over two ranges to Bishops Castle, or south to Knighton, passing on the way the delectable Chapel Lawn Valley. Hence to go from Brampton Bryan to

PLATE VI.

FOUR OF THE "TWELVE APOSTLES," BROMFIELD

VIEW OF BUCKNELL FROM THE SOUTH

PLATE VII.

STOKESAY CASTLE AND CHURCH, FROM THE WEST

THE ENTRANCE FRONT, CONDOVER HALL

Knighton, and then by Clun to Bishops Castle is to enjoy one of the hilliest and most impressive runs in England. But it is a very pleasant road that follows the course of the valley of the River Clun up to Newcastle. Not far up on the hills is Bettws y Crwyn, where the church has a fine screen, and the pews are painted with the names of the houses. The poetically named "Hall of the Forest" is, however, but a rather gaunt farm. The road continues climbing higher and higher, practically bisecting the mighty bulge of Clun Forest till it breasts the top of the ridge at Kerry Pole. The way swings round to the left to avoid the last ascent, but everyone should walk up the little rise to enjoy the splendid view. On the right an undulating track, practicable for cycles, forms for some distance a boundary between England and Wales, and leads back to Bishops Castle ; it would be difficult to write too highly of the grandeur of its views. A rough track which leads down from the topmost point passes by a stunted pine wood, where in the season the rambler may enjoy a feast of wonderful wild raspberries. The traveller is now in Wales, and we can only wish him a safe descent down the tremendous steep drop which lands him at Kerry and on to Newtown, Montgomery.

Leaving Clun and its setting of what the folk thereabouts call "dizzy" country, you go eastward again to Craven Arms, natural centre of roadways, unless you first make another detour to Bishops Castle for the reward of a quaint border town and further glorious scenery. It is only a few minutes run from Craven Arms to the village of Stokesay and Stokesay Castle (Plate VII). On one side the castle and the nearby Norman church are reflected in the broad pool that of old supplied water to the moat ; on the other side is the sixteenth century half-timbered gatehouse, a remarkable structure adorned with elaborate carving. Stokesay Castle has fortunately escaped the hands of modernisers. Outside it is quite intact ; inside, the latest work of any consequence appears in the seventeenth century panelling and carved chimney-piece of the Solar, the upper withdrawing room whence two peep-hole windows look down into the great hall below. The great

33

hall itself is altogether unspoiled. Lighted on both sides by lofty mullioned windows with thirteenth century tracery, it has a splendid open-timbered roof upborne by stout oaken members springing from carved stone corbels.

Roger de Montgomery held Stoke in the days of William the Conqueror; from the Montgomerys it passed to the de Lacys and was bestowed by Walter de Lacy on the Say family, whence the name Stokesay. Reverting to the de Lacys, the last of the line left Stokesay to his son-in-law, John de Verdon, who built the great hall and the other older parts of the house about 1240. About fifty years later Walter de Ludlow had permission to fortify the place and it was probably then that the tower and the courtyard walls were added. Leland says of it, " Stoke-Say belongeth sometime to the Ludlo's, now the Vernons, builded like a Castell." The Vernons were the Vernons of Haddon Hall. In the Civil Wars, Stokesay was held for the King but ultimately fell to the Parliamentarians.

Altogether apart from the natural beauty of its surroundings, Acton Burnell is a treasure because of its architecture and historic associations. The thirteenth century church, a transeptal building without aisles, is a gem from the days of Gothic perfection. Especially interesting is an alabaster monument in the north transept; the figures are those of a knight in armour, his lady in the dress of Queen Elizabeth's time, and their nine children. Above are carved the proper heraldic devices topped by a knight's helm and squirrel crest; beneath is cut the legend: " HIC IACET CORPUS RICHARDI LEE ARMIGERI QUI OBIIT 27° DIE MAII ANNO DONI 1591." Here lies the ancestor of the Lees of Virginia; surely Acton Burnell church ought to be a shrine of pilgrimage to all good Americans.

Nearby is Acton Burnell Castle, " a goodly manor Place, or Castel, iiii myles from Shrewsbyri, wher a Parliament was kepte in a greate Barne. It was first made by one Burnell, a Byshope." This was Robert Burnell, chaplain and private secretary to King Edward I, and afterwards Bishop of Bath and Wells as well as Lord Treasurer and Chancellor of the realm. In 1284 he built the castle whose ruddy sandstone ruins, now partly shrouded with ivy, still shew traces of thirteenth century geometrical tracery in the window openings. Like Stokesay Castle, it seems to have been a fortified manor house rather than the usual type of mediaeval castle with moat, drawbridge, portcullis and keep.

The " greate Barne " " wher a Parliament was kepte " is hard by, that is to say, what there is left of it—two massive stone gable ends of what was once the great hall of the original castle, a structure of perhaps Norman date.

Fig. 6.—Pitchford Hall.

Drawn by E. L. Wratten.

There, in 1283, for the first time sate Lords and Commons together in parliamentary council, and there they enacted the *Statutum de Mercatoribus* or " Statute of Acton Burnell," as it is often called. Ancient cedars of Lebanon, elms and oaks cast their protecting shade about these venerable relics of a great past; beyond is a stretch of park; and beyond that, again, rises the steep slope of a heavily wooded hill.

Only a few miles distant, nestling under the lee of a lofty hillside forest, lies Langley. It was from this home

35

that Colonel Richard Lee went out to America in 1641. Langley Hall itself is gone, but the fine half-timbered sixteenth century gatehouse is still standing, although it now only shelters cattle and poultry and is gradually falling to decay. Nearby is Langley Chapel, no longer used and apparently at one time employed as a shelter for cattle or sheep, but now under the protection of H.M. Office of Works.

Keeping on toward Shrewsbury from Acton Burnell you pass through the village of Pitchford, with Pitchford Hall (Fig. 6) standing on a tree-covered knoll, not far from the road, and the parish church close by with its black oaken effigy of Sir Ralph de Pitchford, who died in 1252. Pitchford Hall was built in the early part of the seventeenth century by William Ottley, High Sheriff of Shropshire and is a splendid specimen of the E-shaped half-timbered Shropshire house of that date. Not far to the west of Pitchford is Condover Hall (Plate VII), a most stately Elizabethan dwelling built by Sir Roger Owen in 1598 and said to have been devised by Master Walter Hancocke, an architect-craftsman of great repute at the time. Only a short distance from Condover is the village of Stapleton whose quiet double storey church boasts a bit of embroidery attributed to the hands of Mary, Queen of Scots.

Soon you come into a plain beside the Severn and cross the river to Wroxeter, old Roman Uriconium, with Shropshire's holy hill, the Wrekin, thrusting up his mighty mass to the east. Uriconium, the "English Pompeii," is gradually yielding its secrets to reward the labour of excavation, but much still remains to be done before we shall be able truly to visualise the Roman city as it was before its destruction by the Saxons towards the end of the fifth century. Wroxeter village, close by the excavated part of Uriconium, has also worthy monuments of antiquity to shew, but one of the most impressive things about it is to see here and there old Roman tiles and bricks and other fragments of indubitably Roman origin incorporated in the fabric of the church and other buildings already marked by hoary age to our modern reckoning.

Says John Leland, " The Towne of Shrewsbury standeth

on a Rocky Hill of Stone of a sad redde Earth, and Severne soe girdeth in all the Towne that, saving a little Peice, it were an Isle." Up and down and round about the contours of the hill wind the streets whose names alone—Wyle Cop, the Mardol, Pride Hill, Grope Lane, Butcher Row, Mardol Head and sundry others—are enough to arouse curiosity and interest. The ancient " reddie way " from London to North Wales comes in at the south-east by the English Bridge, continues through Wyle Cop, the High Street and Mardol and goes out again at the north-west by the Welsh Bridge. The tall corner house in Butcher Row is an exceptionally fine specimen of fifteenth century half-timbering, with a contemporary shop-front. The sad plight of Rowley's Mansion, now used for warehouses, is depressing as you think of what must have been its stately port when William Rowley, draper and alderman of Shrewsbury, built it at the beginning of the seventeenth century. But many other ancient monuments of architectural or historic value have fared better. For example, there is the Market Hall; there is Saint Mary's with its splendid old glass and a mural tablet to Admiral Benbow, that "true patterne" of English courage, who died at Jamaica in 1702; there is the spire and choir of Saint Alkmund's where, " in the year 1533, uppon Twelffe daye, in Shrowsburie, the Dyvyll appearyd . . . when the Preest was at High Masse, with great tempeste and Darknesse, soe that as he passyd through, he mounted upp the Steeple in the sayd churche, tering the wyers of the clocke, and put the prynt of his Clawes uppon the 4th Bell, and tooke one of the pynnacles awaye with him, and for the Tyme stayde all the Bells in the churches within the sayd Towne, that they could neyther toll nor ringe "; there is the Abbey where lies buried that ubiquitous eleventh century worthy, Roger de Montgomery; there is the Castle; there is the Council House with its sixteenth-century half-timbered gate-lodge, once the occasional dwelling of the Lords President of the Council of the Welsh Marches and the lodging of King Charles I, on his visit to Shrewsbury in 1642; there is the Grammar School, now the Free Library and Museum; and there is—but why go on? We started out to ramble through *little-known* England, and Shrewsbury is the one spot from middle to southern Shropshire at all generally familiar to people outside of the county who make a practice of touring about.

However, it will not be amiss to call attention to some notable persons whose connexion with Shrewsbury is too often forgotten beyond the bounds of the town itself. For one, there was Charles Darwin, of whom it is said that as a

Fig. 7.—Dame Alice Penderel
(from a painting at Boscobel).

Drawn by H. T. Timmins.

little boy he was given to inventing amazing yarns in order to create an impression. This habit his elders wisely corrected, not by punishment but by refusing to be astonished as the young romancer hoped they would be. Near the old Grammar School (Plate VIII) is a monument to Darwin recalling the fact that this illustrious son of Shrewsbury was a scholar there. The notorious Judge Jeffreys, subsequently created first Baron Wem, was also a scholar at Shrewsbury Grammar School about the middle of the seventeenth century; as a lad, it is said, he was determined to become a great lawyer, but his father, having a presentiment that he would meet a violent end, wished him to enter a quiet and respectable trade! Going back a century earlier, we find the names of Philip Sidney and Fulk Greville on the rolls; this was when Sir Henry Sidney was Lord President of the Council of the Welsh Marches and lived at Ludlow Castle. Dr. Charles Burney, father of Fanny Burney, and author of the "History of Music," was a native of Shrewsbury.

And you will never regret going eastward from Shrewsbury across the county to see Boscobel House (Fig. 7) with its rich associations with Charles II and the Penderel family; nor will you less regret a faring due westward toward the Welsh border to see the Glyn in Alberbury parish, the house in which that " Olde, Olde, very Olde Man," Thomas Parr, was born in 1483. "Old Parr" lived to the respectable age of 152 years and 9 months— which speaks well for the healthfulness of blessed Shropshire—was left a widower when he was 122, whereupon he married a Welsh woman and, three years later, is recorded to have done penance in Alberbury Church for breaking his marriage vow in an affair with a young woman of the neighbourhood! In 1635 he went to London and saw the King. His Majesty, so the story goes, congratulated the Salopian rival of Methuselah on having lived so long and asked him what else he could boast of. Old Parr, at a loss for memorable events, related his illicit amours for which he had done penance, whereat the King rejoined, " O fie, Thomas, fie! Can you remember nothing but your vices ? "

To return to Ludlow as your Shropshire base of Welsh Borderland wanderings, there are two good southern courses into Herefordshire. You can either take the one of two twin Leominster roads over Ludford Bridge and pursue a pleasant varied way directly into Leominster—the western route by Richard's Castle is the hillier and more picturesque—or, as already mentioned, you can run to Bromfield and Leintwardine. Leaving Leintwardine the first road to the left* will bring you to Wigmore and thence to a succession of remote villages dotting a wondrous country as little frequented as southern Shropshire. The direct road to Wigmore from Ludlow is in itself a route of splendid interest. In its 8½ miles it rises to just over 900 feet and is never unpicturesque. Sweeping round Whitcliff with its view over the town the way mounts steadily through Bringewood Chase, reaches the summit at Mary Knowl, and drops to traverse Pipe Aston, Elton and Long Leinthall. With Leintwardine it makes an excellent

* The second is a wider and easier lane ; the first is a scrap of our old friend Watling Street, narrow, but practicable in spite of warning notices.

triangular tour. North-western Herefordshire in its natural characteristics is much the same as its northern neighbour, although as you go south the county offers a more pastoral and gentle type of landscape with winding, tangled lanes from whose hedges of thorn and holly you suddenly emerge

Fig. 8.—Cottage Topiary, Stretton Sugwas, Herefordshire.

Drawn by Sydney R. Jones.

in some hamlet whose half-timber cottages (Plate VIII) rest behind hedge-barriers of clipped yew surmounted by topiary devices (Fig. 8).

To do anything like justice, however, to the hill country of our two counties, it is necessary to leave the main roads and take to some of the innumerable hilly lanes, which will be found equally enjoyable in themselves and in the scenes to which they conduct. In fact you must wander afoot by upland tracks if you hope to penetrate into the heart of the

PLATE VIII.

THE OLD GRAMMAR SCHOOL, SHREWSBURY

(NOW THE FREE LIBRARY AND MUSEUM)

A HEREFORDSHIRE VILLAGE: STOKE PRIOR

PLATE IX.

THE DOVECOTE AND THE RIVER ARROW, EARDISLAND

THE WAY TO THE CHURCH, WIGMORE

country; the actual walking distance may be kept quite short.

Space permits us to refer to only one area, but many are scattered about the ridges and ranges of southern Shropshire and north Herefordshire, and all will repay any sort of exploration. Let us look for a moment at the lozenge-shaped hill stretch contained between Ludlow, Bircher, on the Leominster - Ludlow road by Richard's Castle, Mortimer's Cross, and Wigmore, on the Leominster - Knighton road. From the pretty half-timber cottages of Orleton, from Bircher, from Yatton or from almost anywhere on the Wigmore - Ludlow or the other three boundary roads the rambler can gain access to a series of long, level-topped ridges from 800 feet to 1,200 feet in height, covered with acres of bracken and coppice, seamed by many accessible paths, and giving a view over all the chief hills of south central Wales, the Border and the West Midlands.

From Bircher, for instance, a good surfaced lane rises gradually northwards and, after a gate, runs by the side of the Common. Take a path to the left, and as you work gently but steadily up, the flatter country of Herefordshire comes into view as a wide, blue, gently undulating wooded expanse, bounded by lesser hills, over which can be seen the line of the Malverns, those "curious bubblings up" as Cobbett quaintly called them, the tremendous long level-looking shelf of the Black Mountains and the twin peaks of the Brecon Beacons.

As you work north, the country south of Ludlow lies at your feet, and you enjoy the finest view of the twin Clees, which are spread out before you in the whole of their expanse. Northward, progress is stayed by a sudden wide deep cleft, filled with little hills and rough slopes, and densely wooded ; but bearing round by a level green track the whole of this is unrolled at your feet, with the cottages of the little village of Leinthall Earls or Little Leinthall at its mouth. As you bear round the face of the hill, the westward view shews Wigmore, Aymestrey, Leintwardine and the whole of the hills from Stretton to Radnor Forest. The hill is not named on the map, but its top is occupied by the great prehistoric hill fortress of Croft Ambrey, the oval enclosure of which is between 900 feet and 1,000 feet high. The great banks and ditches are largely filled with mighty trees, themselves hundreds of years old, and they keep their form in spite of the burrowing of generations of rabbits.

From the edge of the hill a comparatively easy way leads down by three pine clumps to a stony lane, and the

first few cottages of the village of Yatton, which is but a stone's throw from the Leominster-Knighton road between Wigmore and Aymestrey. Or you may follow a long projecting level ridge south-west by a good path through woods high above the Lugg all the way to Mortimer's Cross. It is easy to spend a day without coming down from the hills.

In the country round about Wigmore and Aymestrey the bold ranges of wooded hills look down on the Teme and the Lugg before they seek the lower ground to the east. To-day Wigmore village is a small

Fig. 9.—Wigmore Grange, the Old Abbey Gatehouse.

Drawn by H. T. Timmins.

and inconspicuous place possessed of a charm in inverse ratio to its apparent importance ; its history is long and honourable. It was the seat of the Mortimers and, even after their line died out, it was a place of note.

Half-timbered cottages, set along the highway where it bends, or climbing the rocky lane (Plate IX) to the church, half-smothered in flowers and shrubbery ; the ruins of the old castle, dismantled in 1643 after its siege by the Round-heads ; west, the steep wooded heights of the Wigmore

Rolls ; on its eastern side a triangular plain bounded by the sharp rise to the High Vinnals and Bringewood Chase ; an air of rural quietude—such is Wigmore with its memories of the Mortimers ; of Deerfold Forest, whither the Lollards fled and where Sir John Oldcastle took refuge at Chapelhouse Farm ; and of the great abbey whose half-timbered gatehouse (Fig. 9), now surrounded by farm buildings, bears witness to the size and splendour of the old establishment.

Aymestrey, as well set as Wigmore, is the next village on your way through Wigmore-land before you come into the open country and make for Mortimer's Cross, Eardisland and Pembridge. Eardisland, on the Arrow, is one of the most delightful country spots England has to shew. What with the stream broadening out beside the road into a placid shaded pool whereon rides a fleet of swans ; half-timbered houses with stone chimneys and brick stacks—in the Herefordshire manner—mirrored in its surface ; the mellowed stone bridge spanning the little river ; and, just beyond, the lord of the manor's brick and stone dovecote (Plate IX), its base almost in the Arrow's waters, it would be hard to discover anything more idyllic. Pembridge, on the Arrow, in its own way, is not less engaging than Eardisland though its individuality is totally different. As a matter of fact, you will find no two of these borderland villages alike ; that is one of the joys of exploring. At Pembridge the two most outstanding features are the detached belfry (Plate X) of the church and the old timbered market house (Fig. 10), where lads and lasses would take their stand at hiring fairs. The belfry has a massive octagonal stone base surmounted by a roof octagonal as far as the bell stage. The bell stage is square on plan and is supported from within by four enormous wooden posts ; in the bell stage are a peal of bells and the clock. On its diminishing peaked top is a square lanthorn. The whole structure is unique in appearance and in sharp contrast to the Decorated church, from which it is quite separate. Yarpole, not far distant, has a smaller and simpler version of the separate diminishing timber spire. The market house, as may be seen, is not far from a large half-timbered inn.

From Pembridge it is but a few miles to Weobley, one

of the most typical fifteenth and sixteenth century half-timbered villages of the borderland (Fig. 11).   There are few other villages that have as much "black and white" work; there are few that can compare with Weobley in the diversity and carved decoration of the timbering to be seen in close compass.   An especial gem of this sort is the old school-house (Fig. 12) built by John Abell, that worthy old Herefordshire architect-carpenter whom Charles I appointed "one of His Majesty's carpenters" in

Fig. 10.—The Market House, Pembridge.

Drawn by Sydney R. Jones.

recognition of his services during the siege of Hereford. You will see his work again at Leominster.

Near Weobley is the splendid timber house "The Leys," now a farm, and two timber dovecotes at "The Buttas" and Luntley; Fig. 13 comes from farther south, and is dated 1641.   Its octagonal brick treatment shews the variety in these picturesque little erections.

On the road to Leominster you will not regret stopping for a moment at King's Pyon or at the tidy village of Dilwyn

Fig. 11.—Looking to the Church, Weobley.

Drawn by Sydney R. Jones.

45

with its interesting church. Leominster, like most other towns of any size, has felt the heavy hand of modern " improvement " with a corresponding loss of picturesque quality; nevertheless, there are many fine things left which,

Fig. 12.—Porch of the Old Grammar School, Weobley.

Drawn by Sydney R. Jones.

Heaven send, may continue to be spared. Though the site of Leominster is fairly level, it has the blessing of abundant water, since the Lugg and the Arrow and other streams come together; if the people of Leominster were attached to their curious ducking-stool (Fig. 14), when efficacious

46

correction by that means was in fashion, they certainly had unsurpassed opportunities for making use of it. The Priory church is a particularly noteworthy structure, Norman to begin with and possessing all the noble amplitude of Norman building, and added to and repaired in the manners of succeeding ages. Another interesting building in Leominster is the half-timber market hall built by John Abell. It is no longer a market hall, but now a private dwelling facing the green, and it may still be seen in all the glory of its seventeenth century timber work and carved enrichment. Plate x shews its original position.

To reach one of the least known and likewise one of the most rarely beautiful parts of Herefordshire—and that is saying much—you will have to go south from Leominster to Hereford. Take the secondary main road through Bodenham, England's Gate and Sutton Saint Nicholas. Then, for a part of the way, you will follow the course of the Lugg with an high-hanging wood of oaks on your right, and ancient yews spreading over the margin of the river on your left. You will pass Hampton Court, the ancient castellated seat of the Arkwright family, and many another goodly house that will excite curiosity and intrigue interest.

Fig. 13.—The Dovecote, Much Marcle, Herefordshire.

Drawn by H. Inigo Triggs.

From Hereford you can easily reach your goal, the Golden Valley. It lies right next the upper Wye Valley and yet, for

47

some unaccountable cause, many people fail to cross to the other side of the gentle rise and explore this little land apart invested with a mellow glory all its own. The first stage of your journey from Hereford to this little-known land, whose very name bears the charm of ancient mystery, brings you to Kilpeck Church (Fig. 15), not far from the main road to Monmouth after you pass Saint Devereux. There are some remains of the Norman castle, but the gem of the place is the tiny Norman church, a perfect specimen of richly decorated Romanesque work—just as the Chapel on the Heath in Shropshire is a perfect specimen of severely

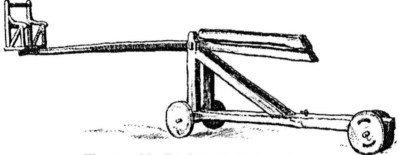

Fig. 14.—The Ducking Stool, Leominster.

Drawn by Sydney R. Jones.

simple Norman fashion—and, even better still, it is absolutely intact and free from the meddling of later centuries.

You can either continue along the Monmouth road to Pontrilas, where Pontrilas Court, a stone country house of Queen Elizabeth's day, is the chief local attraction, and then turn north-west to Ewias Harold; or else you can take a cross road from near Saint Devereux that will bring you directly to Abbey Dore, which derives its name from the valley. As the story goes, when the Normans came into the land and found the stream in the valley called by the Gaelic generic name "Dwr," they turned it into what had the familiar sound to them of "Val d'Or," which became the Vallis Aurea of the monks—hence the English translation, Golden Valley. The Abbey of Dore (Plate XI) was a Cistercian foundation in Norman times and was a large community, as may be easily imagined from what

PLATE X.

THE BELFRY AND CHURCH, PEMBRIDGE

THE OLD MARKET HALL (NOW THE GRANGE), LEOMINSTER
IN ITS ORIGINAL PLACE

PLATE XI.

ARTHUR'S STONE, DORSTONE

THE CHURCH, ST. MARGARET'S

ABBEY DORE, FROM THE SOUTH-WEST

is left of the magnificent church. When John Leland visited the place early in the sixteenth century, he wrote :

" The broke Dour runneth by the Abbay of Dour ; and there it breakethe, a little above the monasterie, into two armes ; whereof the lesse arme runneth throwghe the monasterie ; the bigger arme levith the Abbay a bowe-shot of on the right hond, or banke ; the confluence is againe hard bynethe the Abbay."

Only the transepts, choir and chapels are left of the church built in the twelfth century ; the rest, along with the cloisters and all the abbey buildings, was pulled down at the Suppression. The plunderers appointed one John Phelyps as incumbent at the " wages " of fifty shillings a year ! As might have been expected, spiritualities and temporalities alike fell into sorry dilapidation. When Phelyps's successor, John Giles, read service of a Sunday, he had to stand under the shelter of an arch to keep the rain off his prayer book. Finally, in the seventeenth century,

Fig. 15.——Kilpeck Church.
Drawn by Roland W. Paul.

the remains were repaired and restored with the addition of a fine Jacobean screen. What there is left of the Abbey church of Dore is probably as fine as anything of the period to be found. Maintenance and restoration funds are sadly needed in the way of assistance to the efforts already being made.

From Abbey Dore your way up the Golden Valley leads you to Bacton and thence to the little church of Saint Margaret's (Plate XI) high up on the hills that go on climbing ever upward to the fastnesses of the Black Mountains in Wales. Nothing could exceed the mystic charm of the prospects during your ascent to this remote spot ; part of the time you are either toiling up or else dropping down deep winding lanes between steep banks crowned by high hedges, and all the time you are gradually rising along a lofty shelf overhanging the valley. Every now and again you come to a break in the banks and hedges, and every time you emerge from the cover of the lanes a different panorama greets your eye——the valley, far below, with its meadows and cornfields and the meandering stream ; the heights of the Welsh mountains looming on your left or more distant views of the hills rolling away to the east and south ; again, an orchard close by the roadside where great bunches of mistletoe cling to the branches ; or, perhaps, an upland common with sheep feeding between the clumps of gorse and bracken. The pride of the tiny austere church of Saint Margaret, with its curious wooden bell-cote, is its capacious carved rood loft, built in the Welsh manner and extending right across the upper part of the chancel arch. It is quite ample enough for all the full ceremonial of reading the gospel according to ancient usage. According to a tablet on the north wall, twenty-three men from this secluded parish went to the Great War, and since it is a region mostly of small holdings each worked by a man and his family, three and twenty men from such a parish meant genuine sacrifice.

From Saint Margaret's you go down again into the valley and on to Vowchurch and Turnastone. The explanation for the curious names of these twin parishes, so tradition has it, is this. Two pious ladies resolved to build a church available for both parishes. However, they could not agree about a site and fell to words. One declared : " I *Vow* I will build my *church*, before you *Turn a stone* of yours." Take this yarn for what it is worth ; at any rate, there are the two churches. Inside Vowchurch is a curious and unique arrangement of stout oak supports rising from the floor to the roof.

The farther you penetrate up the Golden Valley, the more you feel inclined to agree with Rowland Vaughan, of the Vaughans of Bredwardine, who wrote in the sixteenth century, " The Golden Vale, the Lombardy of Herefordshire, the Garden of the old gallants, is the Paradise of all the parts beyond the Severn." What might be called the " capital " of the Golden Valley is Peterchurch, which boasts a beautiful and most unusual, as well as

PLATE XII.

GOODRICH CASTLE FROM THE RIVER

ROSS-ON-WYE : VIEW FROM RIVER

PLATE XIII.

LOWER BROCKHAMPTON HALL, HEREFORDSHIRE

THE MARKET HOUSE, ROSS

unspoiled, Norman church in four divisions—a nave, a
choir, a *presbyterium*, and an apsidal sacrarium—with an
arch between each.   Herefordshire is a county of remarkably fine yew trees, and the giant yew in the churchyard
of Peterchurch is one of the best.

Near the head of the valley at Dorstone you can see a
mighty cromlech (Plate xi) called " Arthur's   Stone,"
now a National Monument, beside which King Charles I

Fig. 16.—The Market Hall, Ledbury.

once waited for his Scottish cavalry to come up.   Years
ago part of this stone was sacrificed for road-mending,
but it is still more than twenty feet long.   It is not far
hence over the hills to Hay, just across the border in Wales.
From Hay you can easily come back down the Wye
Valley to Hereford.

Before leaving Herefordshire, amongst other places that
ought not to be missed, though somewhat out of the
usual line of travel, are Ledbury and Goodrich Castle.
Lying at the very foot of the Malvern Hills, on the eastern
boundary of the county, Ledbury, though a sizeable town,

is somewhat away from the main courses of road traffic
and is therefore not so generally well known as might
be imagined from its size. But, however pressing time
may be, you always pause for two things—a look at the
old timbered market hall (Fig. 16), built, it is said, by John
Abell, and standing on sixteen buxom columns of chestnut
where the High Street widens out in the centre of the
town; and a walk up the passage (Plate xiv) to the fine
church which embodies much of the best of Norman,
Early English and Decorated work.

Goodrich Castle (Plate xii) is in the Wye Valley, not
far from Ross (Plates xii and xiii), but somewhat apart
from the course generally pursued by Wye Valley pilgrims.
The church calls up memories of Dean Swift's family, for
several centuries. His grandfather was ejected from the
living for too loyal adherence to King Charles. The
Dean himself gave the church a handsome silver chalice
in 1726.

"One half hath not been told" of the less known parts
of Shropshire and Herefordshire. One is more than loath
to leave these delectable counties, but others challenge our
time and we must be off to them.

CHAPTER II

THE ROLLING UPLANDS

A Passing Glance at the Cotswolds in Gloucestershire and Oxfordshire

Cheltenham — Owlpen — Bibury — Burford — Bourton-on-the-Water —The Swells and Slaughters—Stow-on-the-Wold—Chipping Campden—Bourton-on-the-Hill.

ON first thought, it would seem that not much of either Gloucestershire or Oxfordshire could be spoken of as *little-known* England ; yet there are not a few places in the Cotswold region—not a few places, for the matter of that, *not* in the Cotswolds—that the majority of folk pass by or near without dreaming how much of beauty or historic interest they are missing.

For a starting point you might take Cheltenham. Cheltenham, of course, is perfectly *well* known, but how many who will tell you they know Cheltenham have ever taken the pains to explore the interior of the Montpellier Rotonda and see the furniture that Papworth designed for the Pump Room? Though shabby, it is a great aid to visualising Cheltenham in its palmy days as a spa. How many who say they know Cheltenham have ever been inside the Pittville Pump Room or gone up to the outside of the dome to look away towards Gloucester, or Cleeve Hill or Tewkesbury?

A pleasanter faring into the hills from Cheltenham you could scarcely ask than along the road south-westward towards Painswick. You have wooded hills, precipitous combes and deep dales now on one side of you, now on the other. Paradise—not ill-named—lies half-way down a narrow combe at your left, and the little pub above, by the roadside, is fitly enough called *Adam and Eve*. When you reach Painswick, you will find a delightful as well as typical Gloucestershire church (Plate xiv). You will also find a

53

churchyard with carefully marshalled and trimmed yews that refuse to look sombre, fine tombstones, and a pair of iron stocks. Furthermore, you will find a sunny Cotswold town full of characteristic Cotswold buildings.

After pushing on to Stroud, perhaps you may feel minded to turn aside to Amberley and enjoy a bit of Cots-

Fig. 17.—The Entrance, Owlpen Manor House.

Drawn by Sydney R. Jones.

wold hill and valley country that can hold its own with any of the region. If Amberley does not call you, keep on through Nailsworth and make for Owlpen (Fig. 17) to see a perfect and unspoiled Cotswold manor house and garden of the early seventeenth century. Save a slight addition at one end, early in the eighteenth century, nothing

HALF-TIMBER HOUSES IN CHURCH LANE, LEDBURY

THE CHURCH, PAINSWICK

PLATE XIV.

PLATE XV.

SAPPERTON CHURCH AND VILLAGE

THE THAMES AT KEMPSFORD

had been done to Owlpen since the house was built in 1615, until several years ago. Then only necessary repairs were made to render the house once more habitable; the garden, with its open-air ball-room and other topiary creations (Fig. 18), has never been molested. These walls are about fifteen feet high of mingled yew and box, three feet or more thick, so even that they look as though formed in a mould, and so dense that leaning hard against them makes practically no impression. Owlpen is planted at the foot of a steep hill with a thick wood hanging on its top; facing upon a narrow meadow at the bottom of a bowl-like combe, the house is so shielded by converging hillsides that it is quite hidden till you come directly upon it on falling down a deep lane.

Fig. 18.—Cut Yews, Owlpen Manor.

Drawn by Sydney R. Jones.

The roads from Nailsworth are difficult and will tax both engine and brakes, but the country with its distant views over the Vales of Gloucester and Berkeley far below is well worth it. You will also get a fair notion of the tumultuously tumbled land at the south-west end of the Cotswolds. If your car balks at stiff hill work, you will have to go round by the low road from Stroud through Dursley

55

where Anna Regina in full regalia guards the town from the arcaded market hall; even then you will have some stiff hills.

Just now, on leaving Owlpen, you started for Bibury (Plate xvi)—some distance away. Get out your ordnance map and take any of the roads that will bring you to Cirencester. When you come to Cirencester, leaving the village of Sapperton (Plate xv) to the right among its wooded hills, learn how to call the name of the town, if you don't already know. It isn't as long as it looks in print. And please don't call it "Siren." From Cirencester go out by the ancient Fosse Way and then branch to the right on the road to Aldsworth and Burford. That will bring you straight to Bibury and its long stone bridge across the meadow and the River Coln.

From Cirencester starts the country of the infant Thames, the first stretch of which winds by Cricklade down to Lechlade and near Fairford. Reasons of space forbid us dealing with this district as we should like but we illustrate Coleswell Mill (Plate xvi), one of the first on the stripling river, and the village of Kempsford (Plate xv) on the borders of Wiltshire.

Coming from Cirencester, just as you drop down the hill and turn a bend of the road, there is Bibury ahead of you. To the left, by the mill-race, is a great stone mill with heavily buttressed walls. Directly before you is the bridge across the greenest of water meadows cut by streams, the Coln rippling along its farther side. At the opposite end of the bridge, with only the width of the road between it and the bridge head, is the White Swan Inn seeming to tread on the very toes of the steep wooded cliff-like hill against which it is set. Separated from the inn by the river is a diminutive island garden beside the bridge-end where you can lunch or have your tea in the shade with the purl of the water for music. Beyond the White Swan, and facing the river, a row of stone cottages nestles under the lee of the hill. At the far end of the meadow, to the right, "Arlington Row," a chain of weathered stone cottages lately acquired for the National Trust, meanders toward the hill, the footway before the cottage doors edged by the mill-race hastening to join its parent Coln.

PLATE XVI.

THE BRIDGE AND "SWAN" INN, BIBURY

COLESWELL MILL AND VILLAGE

PLATE XVII.

THE PORCH, NORTHLEACH CHURCH

BURFORD, LOOKING DOWN THE STREET

Such is this Cotswold beauty spot, full of flowers, great oaks, yews and beeches ; full of the music of running water and the hum of bees ; full of sunshine, gleaming on its emerald meadow, bounded by cottages full of simple, kindly folk, as such a place should be.   It is one of those idyllic villages, like Clee Saint Margaret's in Shropshire, that seems to have stepped out of a fairy-book.   One gets nervy about the future of villages like Bibury ; fortunately it is not on a main artery of traffic.

From Bibury you can follow a by-way along the river past Ablington to Coln Saint Denis and rejoin the Fosse Way nearby, or you can go on by the Burford road to Aldsworth and strike off across the downs to Northleach, or you can keep right on to Burford (Plate xvii), " the grey old town on the lonely down."   At Burford you will find plenty to engage you whether your interests lie in the direction of architecture, or sketching, or history, or the everyday life of a market town.   The church is one of the most splendid in Oxfordshire, for Burford was once a very great wool town and the wealthy merchants as well as the nobility gave generously to its building and maintenance. Nor should you ignore Simon Wisdom's Grammar School and Warwick's Almshouses hard by the church, or what is left of Burford Priory, a place full of association with Lucius Cary, second Viscount Falkland.

Like most of the Cotswold towns and villages, it is not built at the top of the hill but lies comfortably near the bottom.   As you cross the high-lying hill roads across the Cotswolds, you can look down on the villages in the combes and on the hillsides, and this habitual snug setting has much to do with their fascination.   Stow-on-the-Wold is the only Cotswold town set on the hill tops—though several others are high-lying—and Stow is bleak ; has always been considered so, if we may trust the old couplet:

" Stow-on-the-Wold,
Where the wind blows cold."

And nigh to Burford is another low-lying village, Swinbrook, most pleasantly set in a dale and possessing a church with some amazing and amusing sepulchral sculpture.

57

But the chief joy in going to Swinbrook is to cross the stile by the church and go across a field—the only way—to an ancient chapel with fourteenth century wall paintings and, in the chancel, part of the tessellated paving of the Roman villa on whose site it was built.

By which road you come to Northleach—whether from Burford or from Coln Saint Denis along the Fosse way—matters not. The one thing to see at Northleach is the church (Plate xvii). Like nearly all the other great Cotswold churches, it is built of wool, so to speak. This means to say that they were chiefly built by the munificence of the fifteenth century wool merchants who had amassed their fortunes from the fleeces of the sheep that fed on the Cotswold downs. Northleach Church has one of the finest if not, indeed, the finest Perpendicular porch in the western Midlands with a chamber above. There are also some fine brasses and several architectural characteristics peculiar to the neighbourhood. Northleach is a somewhat dour village, and apart from the church, there is little cause to linger. This is not at all the case with the next village along the Fosse Way, Bourton-on-the-Water, sometimes referred to as the " Venice of the Cotswolds," thanks to the presence of the Windrush which, rising at Cutsdean, leaves its reeds and rushes and shady trout pools, turns a mill and then moves on gaily between ordered banks beside the village High Street. A passage through Bourton-on-the-Water (Plate xviii) always calls to mind Adam de Saint Victor and the lines of the hymn :

" Right through her streets, with pleasing sound,
    The living waters flow."

The Windrush runs through the middle of the village green and trim little camel-backed stone bridges span the stream. The Manor House, Harington House and several others uphold its claim to architectural distinction, quite apart from the quality of the cottages.

Three villages in the neighbourhood of Bourton-on-the-Water invite both exploration and leisurely dalliance—if you are an artist you will probably have to be dragged away. Two of them, Lower and Upper Slaughter, are to

PLATE XVIII.

LOWER SLAUGHTER VILLAGE

BOURTON-ON-THE-WATER

PLATE XIX.

UPPER SLAUGHTER

Drawn by W. Curtis Green, A.R.A.

THE MANOR, UPPER SWELL

be numbered amongst the " water villages " of the Cotswolds. At Lower Slaughter (Plate xviii) the brook, which later joins the Windrush, is to all intents and purposes the village street. At each side, between the water and the houses, is a narrow roadway little wider than a footpath and small footbridges facilitate neighbourly intercourse.

Upper Slaughter, too, has plenty of water, though the arrangement of the village is altogether different ; here, too, the rambling cottages, with their setting of hill and water are equally attractive. Furthermore, Upper Slaughter can boast of its Elizabethan Manor House with a fifteenth century basement, one of the finest in the Cotswolds. The name *Slaughter*, though it may sound at first rather bloodthirsty, becomes far more agreeable when you realise that it is a corruption of *sloe tree*. When Domesday Book was compiled the place was set down as *Slotre* manor, presumably from the presence of a particular sloe tree as a landmark or boundary, and, in the course of centuries, *Slotre* became *Slaughter*.

At Upper Swell you will see close together a typical little Norman church and a small Manor House (Plate xix) of unusual beauty. Unlike the great late Cotswold churches in the larger centres, the churches in the smaller and less opulent communities remained very generally Norman or Early English, with occasional slight alterations or additions. The Manor House at Upper Swell is of early Stuart date, and, though now a farmhouse, has escaped those mutilations so frequent when the lord moves out and the farmer moves in.

Though Stow be known as the bleak town of the Cotswolds, it by no means follows that it is lacking in things worth seeing. As a matter of fact, Stow rarely gets full credit because most people merely pass through on their way without stopping. That, perhaps, is the penalty it pays as the meeting place of so many roads ; it suffers the anomaly of being *little known* because everybody accepts it as a matter of course without concerning themselves to investigate its real character. The town is the nerve-centre, so to speak, of the main road systems across the Cotswolds. No less than six important main roads converge there—the road to Evesham and Worcester, the road to Cheltenham and Gloucester, the road to Tewkesbury, the road to Stratford-upon-Avon and Birmingham, the road to Banbury; and finally the Fosse Way leading to Cirencester and Bath, from which, just at the foot of Stow Hill, the road to Burford and Oxford branches off so that Stow is *really* at the junction of seven roads rather than six.

Such a position at the crossing point of so many important highways for centuries, was bound to have a marked effect on the town's history. For one thing, Edward IV granted Stow a charter to hold a fair twice a year—on May 1st, the Feast of Saint Philip and Saint James, and on October 13th, the Feast of the Translation of Edward the Confessor. When the New Style was adopted the fair was held on the 12th of May and the 24th of October. Stow Fair was at one time one of the largest and most famous in this part of England; now it is no longer what it used to be. It is still held, but it has long been chiefly a horse fair, though cattle and sheep also are sold and there is still a fringe of " attractions " to catch the pennies of the crowd. Droves of half-wild ponies are brought all the way from Wales, as well as horses from a less distance, and you can often hear the Gaelic spoken if you go through Stow at fair time. Sometimes all the roads are so full of horses, ponies and cattle going to or coming from the fair that driving is interrupted.

Stow Church was rebuilt in the thirteenth century and it was then that Edward the Confessor was taken as patron saint in place of an earlier dedication to a local hermit of the same name who is said to have founded the church in the ninth century; down to the sixteenth century the town was called Stow Saint Edward. Over the altar hangs rather a fine Crucifixion by Gaspar Crayer, a pupil of Rubens. Outside, at the end of the market square, the old stocks are still to be seen and there are the remains of an ancient market cross. At Stow was fought the last open fight of the Civil Wars and it was here that the venerable Lord Astley laid down his arms.

From Stow to Chipping Campden (Plate xxi) is but a few miles. Your best way will be by the Worcester road, then turn to the right at the "Four Cross Hands," an ancient finger-post at the cross-roads before you reach the top of Broadway Hill, and drop down Westington Hill into the town. Chipping Campden is one of the Cotswolds' finest treasures, an ancient "wool" town (Plate xx) which, thanks to its position in a fold of the hills aside from the main traffic currents has remained unspoiled and little changed for the past three centuries. To be seen it must be made the object of a special visit.

Chipping Campden's greatest glory is its church, rebuilt about the middle of the fifteenth century by the munificent piety of the wool merchants. One of the most considerable, William Grevel, had left a bequest in 1401 and had already taken an active part in preparing for the reconstruction. The present tower he had finished before his death. The church contains also a fourteenth century crimson velvet cope, powdered with gold stars and crowns, and possessing richly embroidered orphreys and hood; and beautifully embroidered altar hangings, probably the only complete set of that date remaining. These hangings were reproduced for the altar of Westminster Abbey at the Coronation of the King and Queen in 1911.

William Grevel's house is still standing in the High Street, marked by its singularly handsome Gothic bay, two storeys in height. Across the street is the fourteenth century Woolstaplers' Hall, now used as a dwelling, and a little below is the early seventeenth century market hall which appears in one of the illustrations. The church (Plate xxi) is at the eastern end of the town; its exquisite tower draws like a magnet. On the way to the church, you pass the Almshouses (Plate xxi), of such charming aspect that you would almost be reconciled to abject poverty to be able to live in one of them; by the seventeenth century endowment of the founder, Viscount Campden, the pensioners all have allowances annually for coals, clothing and food.

At the south side of the church is the old gateway to Campden House. The gateway is now walled up and there is nothing left of this noble mansion of early Stuart days save a ruined arch and its piers, the little detached banqueting house with its moulded stone chimneys, " the Almonry " and the barns. The house itself was burned down in May, 1645, by Sir Henry Bard when he left it with his Royalist garrison to aid in the relief of the siege of Chester. This he did to prevent its falling into the hands of the Roundheads. The plan of the house, as well as the plan of the old gardens, can still be traced.*

To the north-west of Chipping Campden is Dover's Hill, so-called because of the Whitsuntide games and sports held there on a grassy plateau near the summit at the instance of Robert Dover. Outraged at the Puritan attack on old English outdoor pastimes, the abandonment of which he said drove the country folk to the pot-house, and

> " being full of activity and of a generous free and public spirit, he did with leave from K. Jami, select a place on Cotswold Hills in Gloucestershire, where those Games should be acted. Endymion Porter Esq, a Native of that County (he was Lord of the Manor of Aston Subedge, nearby) and a Servant of that King, a Person also of a most generous Spirit, did, to encourage Dover, give him some of the King's old Cloaths, with a Hat and Feather and Ruff, purposely to grace him, and consequently the Solemnity."

" Dover's Meeting," as it was called, was a great success and not only the country-folk, for whom it was founded, but also the nobility and gentry from sixty miles around resorted thither. It was held regularly till, as Wood says, " the rascally Rebellion was begun by the Presbyterians, which gave a stop to their Proceedings, and spoiled all that was generous or ingenious elsewhere." At the Restoration, however, the annual games were revived and the meeting continued to be held every year till 1851, at which time such a rowdy element had come to frequent the sports that the merrymaking was permanently discontinued.

Leaving Campden by the road to Mickleton and Stratford-upon-Avon, you drop down the hill first to Aston Subedge

---

* The only known representation of the great house is a contemporary drawing in the British Museum ; a sketch from it appears in *The Manor-houses of England*, by Jones and Ditchfield, 1910.

PLATE XX.

A COTSWOLD SHEEP MARKET, CHIPPING CAMPDEN

WOOL AT THE FAIR, CHIPPING CAMPDEN

PLATE XXI.

THE STOUR AT CHIPPING CAMPDEN

THE ALMSHOUSES, CHIPPING CAMPDEN

(which is the East town under the edge of the Cotswolds), and then turn left, skirting the foot of the hills, through Weston Subedge and Willersey, passing by a road that leads up into a tiny fold of the hills where hides the hamlet of Saintbury, guarding the tomb and memory of one of the great humanists of the New Learning, the friend of Erasmus, Grocyn, and Linacre. All of these villages are gems and too fine to be dismissed with merely passing mention, but they are fairly well-known to visitors to Stratford and Broadway. What you have missed by turning aside to Chipping Campden is the glorious view from the top of Broadway Hill to the Malvern Hills, the mountains of Wales, the Clee Hills and the Wrekin, to say nothing of the Vale of Evesham spread at your feet; likewise you have missed the descent into the village and all the incidents there to be seen. But, again, these cannot be counted as little-known.

Passing by Broadway, or rather through the lower end of the village, you continue to the left by the Cheltenham road, still skirting the western foot of the hills. Thus you come to Buckland, where the little great-hall of the present Rectory with its angel-carved hammer-beam roof is an almost intact and perfect treasure of fourteenth century domestic architecture. At Stanton (Plate xxii) the village itself is a vision of beauty and orderliness as well as of representative Cotswold architectural excellence, as at Broadway, though in a different manner and full of its own distinct individuality. For the care with which everything is preserved and maintained, you may thank the present Lord of the Manor. Stanton Court, the church, the *old* Manor house and the Warren House are a few of the special excellences of Stanton, but it is hard to single out any one feature. The natural setting of all these villages lying under the western escarpment of the Cotswolds is lovely beyond description.

At Stanway there is Stanway Court with its marvellous oriel window and its walled gardens, and there is the splendid tithe barn, and there are many things besides that deserve a leisurely visit—things not seen from a car, but demanding unhurried inspection. And while you are at

Stanway, remember that the direct road will take you to Tewkesbury in less than half an hour. Tewkesbury ought really not to be included as little-known because, in the ordinary course, it ought to be *well* known. As a matter of fact, it is surprising to find how few people are familiar with it and how many more know it not, except as a name on the map where Avon joins Severn. The Abbey with its splendid Norman tower, its early glass and its marvellously sculptured chantries ; the Bell Inn, over against the Abbey gates, and its reminiscences of *John Inglesant, Gentleman ;* the old mills, and the timbered houses and old hostelries—though the most obvious, these are not the only things you will find to charm you in Tewkesbury. You may go from Tewkesbury to Cheltenham or Winchcombe, another little wool town with a glorious church, and so reach the road under the Cotswold escarpment, or returning again to the Cotswolds by the same road to Stanway, you push on up Stanway Hill, turn to the left and follow the field road—unless you wish to go back to Stow—and then come out on a road to another hillside village needed to round off your glimpse of little-known Gloucestershire ; Bourton-on-the-Hill, on the London-Worcester Road, not less engaging in its own different way than Bourton-on-the-Water. You come into Bourton-on-the-Hill over the crest of the hilltop and tumble right down the one street. Tumble is the right word to use because the descent is very steep. On the right, below the *Groom and Horses* is the church, compounded of every style from Norman to late Perpendicular. Lower down is the great house, shewing a most decorous late seventeenth century stone front, but really dating from the Middle Ages. Close beside it is another monastic tithe barn that can rival the grace of that at Stanway, though by no means as large. Bourton-on-the-Hill, too, is a place to linger and explore, but the road is before you and, if you are to penetrate the less known retreats of the Chilterns and East Anglia, you must hold on your way to Oxford without further stop, regardless of temptations to turn aside.

CHAPTER III

THE CHALK HILLS

The Berkshire Downs and the Buckinghamshire Wooded Chilterns

Dorchester—Abingdon—Uffington—Down Tracks—Newbury—The Hendreds and Hagbournes—Steventon—Ewelme—Fingest—West Wycombe—Jordans—William Penn—Chalfont St. Giles—Langley—Penn Village—Chenies—Bradenham—Aldbury—Ivinghoe.

IN the scenery and configuration of the land; in the type of domestic architecture ; in the nature of the associations, and in every conceivable way, the differences between the Welsh Borderland and the Cotswold portions of Gloucestershire and Oxfordshire will have become apparent to any ordinarily observant person who has followed somewhat the course outlined. When you enter upon the Berkshire Downs and the Chiltern country, you will find conditions different from those in either the Cotswolds or the Welsh Borderland—not worse or better, more or less pleasant, but simply different. And yet the distance between many of these most unlike places is inconsiderable. Oxford you will probably find a convenient spot as headquarters for your rambles amongst the Berkshire Downs and the Chilterns.

The venerable village of Dorchester-on-Thames, about nine miles from Oxford, is another place which, like Tewkesbury, it seems improper to count amongst little-known places because, by its position, it ought to be well known. It is on one of the main roads between London and Oxford and hundreds pass through it by road every day in the year. Those who travel this road cannot help being familiar with its winding street, its pleasant-fronted houses, and the genial mien of its old hostelries, as well as with the long severity of roof-line displayed by the double-naved Abbey church rising before you as you enter the village by the bridge at the London end. But how many who shoot through like an arrow, or even stop for refreshment at the inns, ever pause to think of the associations bound up with this erstwhile see city and mother of bishoprics? How many ever go into the Abbey and see amongst other riches, the remains of fourteenth century wall painting, the Jesse window, and two other chancel windows with extraordinary and graceful *sculptured* tracery, rare enough and probably the finest known?

In 634, Saint Birinus made Dorchester his See city as Bishop of Wessex, his diocese including Buckinghamshire and a part of Oxfordshire. In 664, Agilbert, the successor of Birinus, retired to Northumbria and Winchester became the only see in Wessex. In 679, when Archbishop Theodore reorganised the bishoprics, he divided the unwieldy Mercian Diocese of Lichfield and re-established the See of Dorchester, consecrating Aetla bishop. After Aetla's death, the Diocese of Dorchester was absorbed into the See of Leicester; this arrangement continued till the ninth century. About 869, because of the Danish domination of the Midlands, the Bishop of Leicester fled to Dorchester, and thence Dorchester remained the See city until the Norman Conquest. The jurisdiction of the Bishops of Dorchester extended over the whole of the Midlands, including Lincolnshire. After the Conquest, during the episcopate of little Bishop Remigius—he was only four feet tall—about 1073 or, perhaps, a few years later, it was decided to make the See city Lincoln; Dorchester, therefore, was not only the predecessor and mother See of many of the Midland dioceses but also the immediate antecedent of the Diocese of Lincoln. After the removal of the bishopric Dorchester rapidly declined in importance until Alexander, Bishop of Lincoln, founded there an Abbey of Augustinian Canons in 1140. Thereafter the history of Dorchester was the history of the Abbey until the Suppression. Dorchester formed part of the Diocese of Lincoln until the Bishopric of Oxford was established in 1541.

Just about a mile from Dorchester, on the Berkshire side of the river, the Wittenham Clumps (Plate XXIV) both

PLATE XXII.

ST. HELEN'S CHURCH AND THE THAMES, ABINGDON

WARREN HOUSE AND STANTON VILLAGE

DUCKING A SCOLD

Printed by T. Rowlandson

A BUCKS LACE MAKER,
LUDGERSHALL.

AN OLD COUNTRY WOMAN,
DORCHESTER

PLATE XXIII.

remind us of the old British hill camps of Sinodun and also serve as landmarks for miles.

With the Wittenham Clumps to the left, the road to Abingdon takes you through softly undulating country, past Clifton Hampden and its small Norman church, dramatically set, past Sutton Courtenay, through fat lowland luxuriance to that time-honoured bridge across the Thames " i-founde " by " King Henry the Fyft in his fourthe yere," and so into the one-time county town of

Fig. 19.—The Barley Mow Inn, Clifton Hampden.

Drawn by C. Patterson.

Berks, ere Reading's biscuits and seeds and other pushful industries snatched away the honour. The Abingdon Monastery was probably destroyed by the Danes. Mr. Belloc says : " It stood right in the marshy and waste spaces of the middle upper River, commanding a difficult but important ford, and holding the gate of what was to be one of the most fruitful and famous of English vales. It can only have been from Abingdon that the culture and energy proceeded which was to build up Northern Berkshire and Oxfordshire between the Saxon and the Danish invasions.

There only was established a sufficient concentration of capital for the work and of knowledge for the application of that wealth."

One knows not whether to call Abingdon well or little-known. Perhaps it would be more diplomatic to evade the issue and say that it is ignored and neglected by both the average tourist and the average motorist off for a week-end. It is even more neglected by the outside world than Dorchester, for fewer people pass through; you don't expect a quiet town to be thronged as Westminster Abbey— that would be too dreadful—but it is hard to see why curiosity, if nothing else, does not impel more folk to linger for a moment over such precious heritages as Christ's Hospital, Saint Helen's Church or the County Hall. Abingdon is full of other good things besides these. If it doesn't especially interest you that Christ's Hospital (Fig. 20) with its curious timbered Tudor cloister dates from the reign of Edward VI, incorporating a much older panelled guild hall of singular beauty, or if wealth of historic association makes no compelling appeal, at least you will find more than enough picturesque comeliness, to which the most untutored sense of appreciation can scarcely be indifferent.

If you are a tree-lover, you will wish to see the mighty elm at Fyfield to which Matthew Arnold alluded in the lines :

" Maidens, who from the distant hamlets come,
    To dance round Fyfield elm in May."

It measures thirty-six feet in circumference and according to local superstition witches resort there to dance about it in their midnight revels. This amiable hamlet also boasts a fourteenth century manor house (Plate xxv) beside the church. If you keep on through the villages of Kingston Bagpuze and Buckland, the Swindon road will bring you to Faringdon. Within Kingston Bagpuze parish is New Bridge, the oldest of all the bridges over Thames, mentioned by Leland as " lying in low meadows, often overflowed with rage of rain." At Buckland House is still preserved Sir John Throckmorton's famous coat, made in 1811, of which you will hear more at Newbury.

At Faringdon the call of the Berkshire Downs prompts you to dip down into the Vale of White Horse to Uffington, lying tangled up in its winding ways in full sight of White Horse Hill. The complicated lanes in and about this straggling village are not without an advantage; they make it easy for one to survey the thatch-roofed clunch cottages and their flower-filled gardens from every angle. The Rectory has close associations with Thomas Hughes,

Fig. 20.—Christ's Hospital, Abingdon.

Drawn by T. Raffles Davison.

the author of *Tom Brown*; in fact, a good portion of the *School Days* and the *Oxford* were written within its walls.

Having extricated yourself from Uffington by-ways spread like the "snares of the fowler," a moderately winding way brings you in to Kingston Lisle at the foot of the steep rise over Lambourn Downs, the south-easterly mass of White Horse Hill (Plate xxv). Here you may take the old Roman road straight before you and, by making only slight detours, pass through Sparsholt and Childrey and thence to Wantage, or you may turn sharp right by a road up over the downs, a road that looks not at all inviting as regards either surface or grade. But if you disregard the road's rebuff and resolutely push up its first stiff climb past a strip of woodland at the left, you will be repaid manifold. Following an unfrequented course that soon dwindles into little better than a rough farm track, you traverse the rise of the downs and then descend the longer southern slope, till you pass the Barrows of the Seven Kings and, not long after, come out on the road to Lambourn. The nature of the trail compels you to go slow and, furthermore, you wish to go slow. Indeed, if you heed inclination, you will stop many times to gaze at the great sweep of the downs. There is no place, perhaps, where the centuries seem more quickly to slip away to the days when Britain was Roman, or earlier still. In a subtle manner the spell of the downs makes you feel curiously close to the men who lie within the Barrows of Kings.

Apart from the beauty and the haunting mystery of it all, a journey like this over White Horse Hill and the Lambourn Downs will make you realise how altogether different is this chalk country from the Welsh borderland, particularly in its characteristic contours. The bold, sweeping, swelling contours of the downland; the delicate curves of the ridge lines; the long, heaving rise of the slopes—all these are full of an immeasurable repose wholly their own. They are utterly unlike the more urgent thrust of the Cotswolds or the dramatic tumult of Southern Shropshire.

Keeping on a few miles from Lambourn will bring you to Newbury, which used to be very well known, but seems to have been forgotten or ignored by most of the present generation except in connexion with races. Yet Newbury has its charms that take little searching to discover. It was a great wool town, and later an important centre of cloth-weaving. It was while cloth and the clothiers were still dominating factors of Newbury that Sir John Throckmorton's famous coat was made in 1811, the coat still preserved at Buckland House. The story of it is this. Sir John once made a bet that the wool growing on a sheep's

THE CAMP ON SINODUN HILL, ABOVE THE WITTENHAMS, LOOKING TO THE BERKSHIRE DOWNS

PLATE XXIV.

PLATE XXV.

FYFIELD MANOR HOUSE

THE WHITE HORSE AND ITS HILL

back in the morning would be a coat by evening. In thirteen hours and twenty minutes, from start to finish, the wool was "shorn, spun, spooled, warped, loomed and woven," the cloth was "burred, milled, dried, sheared and pressed," the coat was made up and Sir John wore it at supper that night.

A pleasant reminder of Newbury's great days remains in the Cloth Hall, now a museum. Built at the beginning of the sixteenth century, it is a small structure with an overhanging upper storey, upborne by exterior columns, and its erection is credited largely to John Smallwood, *alias* Winchcombe, *alias* "Jack of Newbury," a conspicuous character in Newbury annals. He was a wealthy clothier and did much for his town. Beginning as the "good apprentice" he married his master's widow, was host to Henry VIII in Newbury, and ended by achieving knighthood. "Jack of Newbury" died in 1519 and was buried in the fine Perpendicular parish church of Saint Nicholas, of which he was a generous benefactor.

Little of the oldest Newbury is left, but its comely Georgian aspect is gratifying because of many pleasant Classic diversities, and the River Kennet with its bridges (Plate xxvi) and the houses along its banks affords picturesque glimpses. Then, too, there are the rich memories of the battles fought at Newbury during the Civil Wars, and nearby Shaw House, a comely brick Elizabethan mansion, and the remains of Donnington Castle, about both of which the fighting raged, are still to be seen. Just to the west is the hamlet of Speen which had yielded precedence to Newbury (the new Burgh) as early as the time of Edward Confessor.

If, instead of taking the road across the downs from Kingston Lisle towards Lambourn and Newbury, you take the old Roman Way towards Wantage, you will pass for some distance between enormous holly hedges and beneath an avenue of giant elms until you turn left to make a detour through Sparsholt and Childrey, worth making if you value simple, homely beauty. As you come up again from Childrey through a deep cutting to rejoin the Roman road, an unexpected open view of downs and sky suddenly bursts upon you astoundingly. It is like popping up through a trap-door on to the roof of the world.

Wantage, lying at the foot of the Downs, you approach with a feeling of veneration ; it is the birthplace of Alfred the Great, but not even the site of the old palace of the Saxon kings is certainly known. On the thousandth anniversary of his birth, 1849, his statue was set up in the market-place. Wantage has no particular " sights " ; it is just one of those comfortable country towns with hostelries and Georgian-faced houses which, though of no great notability, it is a pleasure to regard and study.

Between Wantage and Wallingford are the Hendreds and the Hagbournes (Plate XXVI), four precious villages set amidst orchards and lying far enough off the highway— a mile or more—to keep them from the clatter and sordidness of the outer world. To reach any one of them you have to make a special little side trip ; you likewise have to turn your back on the twentieth century—which is more or less of a relief—and make an excursion several centuries into the past. The village baker sells his loaves and buns behind latticed casements without feeling constrained to yield to the strident plate glass window, and the purveyor of petrol can do without a blatant display of pumps and enamelled signs. The village cross where the straggling street broadens out and makes a bend ; the parish church, half-hid behind its screen of yews ; the thatched cottages with walls of mellow patterned bricks of variant tone and latticed casement windows, or timber-built with overhanging upper storeys and weathered parging of hues from salmon to ochre brown ; the gardens with their colours, the surrounding orchards, the hedges of thorn with occasional holly or outposts of buxom boxwood—these softly gentle incidents all unite to make the Hendreds and the Hagbournes veritable idylls of British rural life. Garden walls of cob, with peaked thatch capping, along the lanes in this Berkshire elysium strengthen the reminiscence of Kate Greenaway coloured illustrations. Not far away are other villages—Harwell, Blewbury, Aston Tirrold and the like—of much the same unspoiled charm and little-known because they lie to one side or the other of the accustomed arteries of traffic and, like the Hendreds and the Hagbournes, you can and do pass most of them without suspecting their existence. Their aloofness has been their salvation.

From this unequalled group of villages with their old houses of distinctive and beautiful craftsmanship, Steventon stands apart by situation and character. It is rather north on more level ground and is the first station beyond Didcot on the G.W.R. Bath line, but fortunately neither rail track nor station obtrude themselves unnecessarily. After a fringe of rather modern houses the road through Steventon swings across a wide green, where the way is bordered by young chestnut trees, a mass of pink blossom in May. Though the green is delightful the houses are rather modern, but once you have turned to the left there is a beautiful group of houses of the most distinctive Berkshire craftsman-ship, in which most varieties of building and roofing material seem to be represented. Scattered cottages and isolated farms push themselves forward to the road or stand back among green willow trees; one of the finest examples was gutted by fire in August 1929. There is a barn surmounted by a dovecote, and one extremely pictur-esque row has some examples of plain pargetting (Fig. 21), and the local bays and oriels in their full character. A remarkable feature is the Causeway, for the maintenance of which it is said two sisters left a yearly sum. In the middle by a little green some rough stone steps lead to a narrow raised cobbled footway some feet above the rest of the ground. It is difficult to imagine that floods necessitated its making, but between its rows of pollarded lime trees it is wholly delightful.

From East Hagbourne a few miles along the Port Way will bring you to Wallingford where you cross Thames and plunge into the Chiltern country. Wallingford, scarcely little-known but rather neglected, lives on in contented tidiness, indifferent to the carelessness of the passing world and wrapped in its proud and pleasant memories of loyalty to the King's cause to the very last in the Civil Wars, or those earlier memories of sheltering Queen Maude when she escaped thither over the snow from Oxford, wearing a white cloak, and from the castle held Stephen at bay till relief came. The castle is utterly gone, thanks to the Cromwellians for finishing its ruin, and nought but the site is left to remind you of Queen Maude, the Treaty of Wallingford or the gallant stand of the King's upholders against the Roundheads. Incidentally, it is worth remembering that between Wallingford and Windsor you will find some of the loveliest stretches of river scenery along the

Fig. 21.—A Pargetted House at Steventon.

Drawn by Sydney R. Jones.

whole length of Thames, especially where the windings of the stream cut between the outlying rises of the Berkshire Downs and the Chilterns (Plate XXVII). It is not for us to escort the traveller up or down the " Stream of pleasure," which can scarcely rank as little-known, but as we have pictured typical Border or Cotswold buildings, we here illustrate mills and farm buildings (Plates XXVII and XXVIII) in the Thames Valley district, which

PLATE XXVI.

A BRIDGE AT NEWBURY

EAST HAGBOURNE CROSS AND CHURCH

PLATE XXVII.

THE RIVER THAMES AT HART'S WOOD

A THATCHED BARN, MOULSFORD VILLAGE

exemplify the truth that there need be no divorce between the utilitarian and the picturesque.

From Wallingford, if you are wise you can follow by-ways to Ewelme. Whatever else is omitted a visit should certainly be paid to Ewelme, which lies on the lower slopes of the Chilterns as they die down towards the River Thames, from which the way to it runs by the side of a whole series of watercress beds, a brilliant mass of white flowers in spring.

Ewelme can also be reached by a steep drop from the higher plateau at Cookley Green through the gap in the hills at Swyncombe, and the old Icknield Way, sometimes a modern lane, but more often a wide winding green track at the foot of the steep escarpment, passes diagonally within a short distance.

The roads through the village divide and rejoin to make a sort of oval which is placed, however, on quite a steep slope, and round and between this figure lies the village itself. The cottages and houses are short and diverse— plastered walls and thatch, and Georgian brick, a picturesque scene in varied stages, but the chief group, one of the most pleasant and gracious in England, is the old parish church, linked on to the quadrangular fifteenth century almshouses, built in red brick, and adjoining the school, in the same material.

The Chaucer family have left their mark on Ewelme. Thomas Chaucer, son of the poet, was Speaker of the House of Commons and Steward of the Chiltern Hundreds, and obtained possession of Ewelme through marriage. His daughter Alice, whose name survives in Dame Alice Farm, near Watlington, married for the second time William de la Pole, 4th Earl of Suffolk, who after many vicissitudes at the time of the Wars of the Roses was put to death at sea when his ship was intercepted on the way to France. His son married Elizabeth Plantagenet, sister of Edward IV, and lived in the Palace at Ewelme, of which scarcely a stone remains.

The little quadrangle of the Almshouses, though restored, is delightful, with a covered walk around the well in the centre of the court, and above it half-timber dormers with herring-bone brickwork. From the almshouses a steep flight of steps leads to the parish church, rebuilt during the lifetime of Dame Alice in 1475. The steps are worn hollow with the feet of generations of the inhabitants of the almshouses. The interior has plain but fine roofs, and is a repository of the richest late mediaeval craftsmanship. The fretted font-cover soars to the roof and is surmounted by a delightful little feathered angel. A local squire, Colonel Francis Martyn, who stood high in Cromwell's favour, successfully intervened to prevent the destruction of the monuments during the unsettlement of the Civil War, but a booby of an early 19th century rector replaced the whole of the rest of the nave woodwork with sham Gothic productions, which he no doubt considered a vast improvement.

The Chapel of the Almshouses, south of the Chancel, has a rich panelled roof with infinite repetitions of the sacred monogram and carved angels at every corner. There is a brass to Thomas Chaucer and his wife who died in 1436, and another Chaucer tomb is bright with many-coloured heraldic shields. But the supreme glory of the church is the alabaster monument of the Duchess of Suffolk herself, who died in 1477. Her effigy lies in stately dignity, with splendid tabernacle work above her head and little angels to smooth her pillow. The rich canopy above has a row of angels, and wooden figures surmount the pinnacles. The alabaster row of shield-bearing angels are of the finest Nottingham work, and through the open tracery of the lowest part of the tomb may be seen—if you do not mind stretching on the floor—the Duchess's effigy in skeleton form, a pendant to the robed figure above. But it is unprofitable to describe the tomb in detail; you must see it for yourself.

We are now in the Oxfordshire Chilterns, a well-marked area placed roughly in the quadrilateral with Wallingford, Princes Risborough, High Wycombe and Marlow; they contain many places and features of interest. The rambling traveller will enjoy hunting them for himself, and though a fast car can rush across the compact little district in an hour, days may be spent in enjoyable exploration. Remember that the Chiltern's indigenous industry of chair-turning (p. 79) is always of interest, and a local worker can usually with a little persuasion be coaxed to turn a chair leg as a memento in your presence in his shed. At Ibstone, North End, and Russell's Water are wide commons, covered with gorse or bracken, which rival most in Surrey. There are " Scrubs " (go and find out what they are) at Sprig's Alley and Maidensgrove. Wide views over the Vale can be seen especially at Chinnor Hill, all along the road from Aston Hill to Howe Hill, and at Britwell Hill.

In among the hill folds themselves there is an incomparable view of the whole private Wormsley valley from North End, after which the lane plunges a good 300 ft. down to Turville ; a prospect almost as fine of the same valley is spread from Wallace Hill near Stokenchurch. And from Capstone Mill above Fingest you get a fine hill cirque (as also at Maidensgrove Scrubs) with the Hambleden valley stretching to Berkshire and the Thames, and the tiled roofs of Turville below your very feet. There is the deer park at Stonor, crossed by a footpath, and Alms Hill adjoining, where motor cyclists try their powers roaring up the steep rough ascent. The little flint apsidal Norman Church of Swyncombe is set in idyllic woodland surroundings ; don't forget also the Lime Avenue at Turville Heath. And always just above the foot of the escarpment the Upper Icknield Way dips and rises as a wide, green, tree-bordered track ; at one point, ' The Warren,' above Bledlow, it swings round on a high shelf, above the tops of the great trees which fill the hollow below.

South of the Oxford road from Henley to Benson is a hill district bounded completely by the great sweeping bend of the Thames. Its slopes are more gentle, and the whole landscape is on a smaller scale. But there are many quiet little hamlets, " Ends " or " Greens," miles of wandering up-and-down lanes, and woods of all sorts. The village of Stoke Row, with its Maharajah's well, is set in great cherry orchards ; even the inn is " The Cherry Tree," just as Maidensgrove has " The Furze Bush."

But let us drop down from one of the ridges by a steep descent, to the green wooded hollow where are the twin hamlets of Turville and Fingest. Once a friend inquired of a rustic the way to Fingest, pronouncing it with a hard ' g.' The man looked at him puzzled, and finally a light broke over his face. He slapped his thigh and said, " Why, you means Vin-jis." Professor Mawer* points out that the name comes from *Thing hyrst*, the wood by the assembly. The term *Thing* is Danish, and Skirmett, a nearby hamlet on the Hambledon road, may be a Danish corruption of " Shire Moot."

Fingest lies in an open space at the foot of a high jutting spur with the hills forming a natural amphitheatre around it. In Fingest the few elements combine in charming composition — the churchyard forms a sort of square green with rows of small lime trees overhanging the graves, many of which have wooden memorials. A few cottages with bright gardens are by the side of a lane, which soon slants across the hill to the Marlow road and goes on into the recesses of the hills. The Fingest Inn, which was evidently built during the reign of Charles II, is appropriate and is kept by hospitable people. The church of St. Bartholomew (Plate XXIX) is the outstanding feature ; its tower dominates the dwellings and stands up boldly when viewed from the high ground towards Ibstone. The great Norman tower is wider than the actual church, and some suggest that it was originally a ' tower nave.' On each of the four sides are twin semi-circular Norman windows and the great width is capped by an 18th century tiled roof in two spans, the inverted double-V giving a curious effect.

From the top of the ascent, at Fingest Grove, you can drop down to the Oxford Road, near West Wycombe (Plate XXIX). The single street, under the green hill surmounted by the Georgian church, with its deserted coaching inns and 15th century " Church Loft " is delectable, and has recently been safeguarded for the nation. The highway to Oxford plunges up Dashwood Hill, robbed of its terrors by regrading, and another road parallels the rail to Princes Risborough, but, an alluring thin lane runs under the hill, charges up a steep

* *Problems of Place Name Study*, 1930.

78

PLATE XXVIII.

THE MILL, STREATLEY ON THAMES

MAPLEDURHAM MILL

PLATE XXIX

FINGEST CHURCH FROM THE SOUTH

THE VILLAGE STREET, WEST WYCOMBE

pitch to Bledlow Ridge, and after threading that long hamlet, tumbles as steeply down to Chinnor in the vale.

From Bledlow ridge you can have a series of the most impressive distant views to the heights across the Princes Risborough valley; from several points here, too, you can see the Whiteleafe cross, while you are near that of Bledlow, Buckinghamshire's two chalk cuttings on the hillsides. Across the valley running up from West Wycombe, on the other ridge, the hamlets of Naphill, Walter's Ash, Lacey Green and Looseley Row make an almost continuous village, seven to eight hundred feet above sea level, offering noble prospects. As you traverse these little-frequented heights you may come upon more than one of the old pole lathes in a shed by the roadside where chair-legs and stretchers are being turned for the furniture factories of High Wycombe. These lathes are of primitive type, but the hill-folk pursue their local industry with prowess handed down from father to son. The old saying "Beat a bush and you start a thief," of the days when the Chilterns were the lurking-place of highwaymen, may indicate the dour disposition attributed to these hill-folk; there is little at present to justify it, though if there are a few spots which occasionally lend a little colour to the suggestion that the local folk are still somewhat rough, we can rejoice that they are well endowed with characteristic British calm. The possibilities of a lively disturbance in which an unlimited supply of chair legs and staves would be available for missiles are rather serious to contemplate!

It is from West Wycombe but three miles of house fringed road, between green wooded slopes, to High Wycombe or, to be strictly correct and give the town its right name, which almost no one ever does, Chipping Wycombe. There you are within easy reach of the D'Israeli and Penn country, to say nothing of the spots associated with John Hampden, Milton, Waller and Burke and other famous personages.

At no great distance from Beaconsfield and by no means a long way from Stoke Poges, with its memories of Gray, is Burnham Beeches (Plate xxx), the splendid remnant of ancient beech forest preserved by the providence of the

Corporation of the City of London (Plate xxx), not perhaps little known, but not perhaps greatly frequented by folk from overseas, the Friends' Meeting House at Jordans, nestling in a sheltered, shady dell is something of an exception amongst the little-known places in the Chilterns. Yet Jordans can scarcely be called well-known, notwithstanding the many reverent and loving visits of Friends, both from England and from overseas, who have contributed to save this foremost shrine of Quakerism and William Penn's burial place from the encroachments of advancing suburbia, as it has escaped a road-maining.

William Penn, colonist, idealist and statesman, seems always to have cherished a deep affection for Jordans, unweakened by his many preoccupations and the crowding events of a troublous life. In 1672, before the Meeting House was built—it was not built till 1689—he had taken in marriage his first wife, Gulielma Springett, " at Chorlewood at a farmhouse called Kings where friends Meetting was then kept being in ye parish of Rickmansworth in ye County of Hertford." Rickmansworth is close to the boundary of Bucks, and Chorleywood, now a separate parish, is in a long promontory of Hertfordshire in Bucks and close to Jordans. The " Meeting " then kept " at Chorlewood " later became Jordans Meeting, so it was really in Jordans Meeting that Penn was married. At Kings farm Penn and his bride lived during the first years of their married life, and the house is still standing, though so much altered and enlarged that they would not recognise it in its present form. In the little graveyard at Jordans, which antedated the building of the Meeting House, William and Guli Penn buried their three children who died at Rickmansworth. When the Meeting House was built, Penn contributed generously toward the cost and, whenever it was possible, there he went to meeting ; and there, when he died, they laid him to rest in the spot he loved. There it is much more fitting he should remain rather than be translated across the Atlantic to the Colony that gave him little but grief and anxiety while he lived. Penn lies beside his first wife, Gulielma ; his second wife, Hannah Callowhill, is buried in the same grave with him, at least according to recent inscriptions on the tombstones. Besides the Meeting House, with its plain whitewashed walls inside and its unpainted deal forms and panelling, and the old barn said to have been built from the timbers of *The Mayflower* when she ceased her voyages to New England, the old houses hard by the Meeting House, especially Stone Dean farm, should not be overlooked in a visit to Jordans, for they are closely bound up with the history of Quakerism and, furthermore, are rich in characteristic Chiltern quality.

From the peaceful calm of Jordans it takes you but a few minutes to drive through fat farming country to Chalfont Saint Peter and Chalfont Saint Giles, the former through its garden colony, Chalfont Park, well on its way towards becoming absorbed as a part of London's great suburban dormitory. Chalfont Saint Giles, however, is still unspoiled and many go there as pilgrims to the house (Plate XXXI) where Milton lived for a time and finished *Paradise Lost*. Here he came in the summer of 1665 to escape the plague in London and here he received the suggestion for *Paradise Regained*. Thomas Ellwood, the Quaker—so the story goes—to whom Milton had given the finished manuscript of *Paradise Lost* to read, returned it to the poet with this comment : " Thou hast here much to say of Paradise Lost, but what hast thou to say of Paradise Found ? "

It is not generally known that when Milton came to Chalfont Saint Giles to escape the plague, Rubens came also. While he occupied the cottage by the mill he painted the walls and ceiling of one of the rooms. The wall paintings, unfortunately, were long ago destroyed, but Britannia still adorns the ceiling.

But Chalfont Saint Giles cannot be regarded as a part of *little-known* England ; we must press on to places that have not the home of a Milton as a magnet. Chalfont Saint Giles is a homely, hospitable village, and has just the same kindly atmosphere as Langley, at the Windsor end of the county—*old* Langley, not the new part which has fallen under the withering hand of suburbia—where we stopped one day at the inn opposite the church. When the landlady brought us our cold beef and bread and cheese in the bar parlour, and was much concerned to make us perfectly comfortable, she asked naïvely whether we would have some "refreshment" too, meaning ale or some other drinkable, a term not ill-chosen. Attached to the church of this Langley Marish (not *Marsh*, but Maries, cf. Stow Maries in Northamptonshire) is the 17th century Kederminster Library in its own little red-brick building, erected in fulfilment of a bequest and full of contemporary learned or "improving" books. But what will most attract the visitor is the series of painted armorial or strapwork panels with which the walls are covered. It is rare to find so complete a scheme of mural decoration in England of that or any other date.

When William Penn named the counties in his Pennsylvania colony, Bucks was naturally one and Buckingham in the new land was long the county seat. Other Buckinghamshire names, too, like Chalfont, were perpetuated overseas, though a number of place-names from outside the county got mixed in as well, and we find Croydon, Boulton and Bristol all close together in the new Bucks beside the banks of the Delaware, while William Penn called his own manor on the Delaware Pennsbury. This repetition of town names across the water may have been due to a sort of latent nostalgia, but it is impossible not to wonder whether physical resemblances between countrysides may not also have helped. There are very many stretches of country closely identical in both, so much so that at times, if you had been previously blindfolded, it would be hard to tell at first which Bucks you were in. To this occasional striking resemblance the Quaker settlers could scarcely have been blind.

From Beaconsfield as a base you will find it convenient to explore little-known parts of the Chilterns as well as the more low-lying places. The lanes and by-ways will bring you without more trouble than occasional steep grades to all the villages and remote hamlets, but you will miss much if you do not take to the foot-paths across the downs and through the woodlands. Northwards lies Amersham (Plate XXXI), as fine and interesting an old townlet as

PLATE XXX.

BURNHAM BEECHES

JORDANS MEETING HOUSE

PLATE XXXI.

THE "THREE CROWNS" INN, AMERSHAM

MILTON'S COTTAGE, CHALFONT ST. GILES

Beaconsfield, and further along the Aylesbury road, past Missenden, is Wendover, with many old houses, just under the Chiltern's steep start. The villages of Penn, Chenies, Hughenden and the Hampdens are at no great distance while, a little farther away, you will readily come to Speen, Great and Little Missenden, and, in the vale, on its Oxfordshire side, Long Crendon, Brill on its 600 ft. hill (Plate xxxii), and many more, all of them possessing varied features, besides manifold historic memories.

The village of Penn, built on a hill not far from Jordans, people often imagine to be so called from some connexion with the great Quaker colonist. Such, however, is not the case ; Penn village held its name long, long before William Penn, who was born in London, came to marry and live in the vicinity, although he was probably a distant relative of the Penns of Penn. Lying on the summit of a sharp ridge commanding distant views, the village is a peaceful place with its old cottages and houses, its picturesque Crown Inn, its fourteenth century church where are buried the Penns of Penn and also six sons of Thomas Penn, "proprietor of Pennsylvania," and nearby, a little down one slope, Penn House surrounded by its thickly wooded park, all lifted high above the busy world; from the church tower on a clear day you can have a fine panorama. It was not far from Penn that Edmund Buike, in 1796, established a school for sixty of the young French nobility whose relatives had perished in the Revolution. This charity of Burke after his death was carried on by the aid of a government grant until the Restoration of 1814.

At Chenies, up above the valley of the Chess and five miles from Chesham, you come upon a most fascinating and unspoiled village green bordered on two sides by a double row of great elm trees, with others shading the roads that cross at the bottom of the green where the orderly cottages are clustered ; at the top of the green, to the right, is the church, chiefly of the fifteenth century but with remains of twelfth century work visible. Directly before you at the crest of the rise is the manor house, with a number of fine brick stacks, already a good deal remodelled in the time of Henry VIII and much rebuilt since. When Froude stopped in the inn at Chenies, in 1879, he wrote of the general aspect of the village, " All is old-fashioned, grave and respectable," but he had no great sympathy with the Russell family, Earls and Dukes of Bedford, who have possessed Chenies since 1526, when John Russell, first Earl of Bedford, married the Sapcote heiress to whom it had come from the Cheyneys. Leland said of the manor house in 1538:

> " The old House of Cheyneis is so translated by Lord Russell, that hath this house in right of his wife, that little or nothing remaineth untranslated ; and a great deal of the house is even newly set up, made of brick and timber."

In 1556, conformably to the will of her husband, the widow of the first Earl built the Russell Chapel which, under guise of a north aisle, is really a second nave and quite dwarfs the rest in importance. Here, on altar tombs, lie all " the house of Russell robed in alabaster and painted." The chapel has overflowed to a supplementary burial plot, partly behind the west wall of the manor house, which is now occupied by a tenant. When the new Woburn Abbey was built in the eighteenth century, Chenies Manor House was allowed to go to decay, so that in 1749 Horace Walpole wrote :

> " There are but piteous fragments of the house remaining, now a farm, built round three sides of a court. It is dropping down, in several places without a roof, but in half the windows are beautiful arms in painted glass. As these are so totally neglected, I propose making a push and begging them of the Duke of Bedford. They would be magnificent for Strawberry Castle."

Part of the house was afterwards restored and rebuilt, but it never got back its original appearance.

Hughenden has its vivid memories of Disraeli and a visit there lures you on to Bradenham where the elder d'Israeli made his home in the evening of his life. It is a delightful village—an irregular row of pleasant cottages along one side of the green, the old church and the ample brick manor house seated close together at the top, at the bottom a farmstead with generous barns and rickyards, and for background a beech-crowned hill. Nor will you find

Great and Little Missenden less inviting, though their charms be of a different sort, while the scattered high hamlets of Great Hampden, sheltered by beech woodlands, have picturesqueness enough, even were they devoid of historic connexion with John Hampden. To the credit of his memory be it said that he would probably have opposed the trial and execution of his King, for his friend and confidant, the rector of Great Hampden, who knew and shared his sentiments, was afterwards thrust out of his Mastership of Catherine Hall, Cambridge, for signing the protest against the trial of the King and denying the legality of a government " without a King or a House of Lords."

Ere leaving the Chiltern country, Ivinghoe and Aldbury, at one side of the county, and Brill, at the other, claim your presence. The difficulty in visiting *little-known* places in England is that the quest often keeps you hopping over considerable spaces with better-known neighbourhoods in between. But, even at the cost of much journeying, the rewards always justify the going. Besides, here, you have the enduring joy of the Chiltern landscape with distant views across the vales, vistas through beech woodlands, sights along the western escarpment of the downs, or intimate glimpses of country and villages still unblighted by certain phases of modern life. Faring along here in the Chilterns, if anywhere, you feel the spell of the " autumn road, the mellow wind," white mist hovering over black hedgerows, " dead leaves in the lane," and other incidents noted in verse by Rupert Brooke ; not least of all the "laughter and inn fires," at the day's end. It was when Brooke used to visit " The Pink and Lily," near Whiteleafe, that he got his feeling for the Chilterns. Then, too, you can take your way through Monks Risborough and Princes Risborough (Plate xxxii) where red brick houses, softened by age, lead to the old Market Hall.

Aldbury, under the lee of the downs with Moneybury Hill rising behind, steeped in the soft quality of the vale, was the original of " Clinton Magna " in Mrs. Humphry Ward's *Story of Bessie Costrell.* For a number of years Mrs. Ward lived at Stocks, a house at the end of the village, and drew upon the neighbourhood for local colour. More

than a century ago, when Stocks belonged to James Adam
Gordon, his friend Sir Walter Scott came to know the
country hereabouts and it is said that from the name of the
nearby Ivinghoe he drew the title for *Ivanhoe*. Ivinghoe
lies on the side of the hill and is fully possessed of charm,
but the chief reward is a climb up Ivinghoe Beacon and a
tramp across the bare hills whence you can look eastward
for miles along the Dunstable Downs and get that sense of
endless, lofty, unimpeded distance that fires imagination
and stimulates the mind.

When you go to Brill (Plate xxxii) you will also see
Upper and Lower Winchendon. Upper Winchendon, as
its name denotes, lies well up on the height; Lower
Winchendon and its neighbour Cuddington are in the vale,
immersed in a remote dairying country whither few visitors
penetrate. The salmon-washed, timbered cottages punctu-
ated here and there with herring-bone filling, the gardens
with hollyhocks, stocks and roses, the grazing meadows
watered by the Thame between its lines of pollard willows,
create a picture of calm contentment. Brill on its hill,
lifted aloft some hundreds of feet above the Vale of
Aylesbury, more remote and no less picturesque than Lower
Winchendon and Cuddington, is one of those places where
you feel you have come to the world's end and that you will
drop off if you go any farther. Of all imaginable spots, it
is the last you would think of as the site of a royal palace.
Yet it is beyond doubt that Edward the Confessor time and
again stayed at his Palace of Brill; that John Lackland once
spent Christmas there; and that during the time of Henry III
alterations and repairs to the " King's house at Brill "
included " a new great chimney to the Queen's great tower
plaistered chamber," along with an " oriel, with a stair
before the door of the Queen's chamber," as well as " new
glass windows with ironwork in the gable of the King's
tower." What a deal of satisfaction it would be to
archæologists and architects if there were only some traces
of this old royal residence still in existence !

PLATE XXXII.

A CHILTERN MARKET TOWN—PRINCES RISBOROUGH

THE UPWARD WAY, BRILL VILLAGE

PLATE XXXIII.

A BROADLAND SCENE, NORFOLK

THE MILL, DENVER, NORFOLK

CHAPTER IV

THE EASTERN COUNTIES

NORFOLK, SUFFOLK AND ESSEX

General features—Quiet scenery—Hempstead—The Rodings—The
Pant Valley—Finchingfield—Pargetting—The Dunmows and the
Flitch—Thaxted—Saffron Walden—Clare—Hawkeden—Hartest
—Bury St. Edmunds—Knettishall Church—Wymondham—
Hingham—Swaffham—King's Lynn—East Dereham—Wells-
next-the-Sea—Cley—Knapton—Southwold—Lavenham— Kersey
—Stoke-by-Nayland—Castle Hedingham.

IF there be one whole large portion of England that can
be accounted as little-known, it is the part comprised in
the three Eastern Counties, that is to say, East Anglia
and Essex. The term " East Anglia and Essex " is used
advisedly. Too often people forget that East Anglia
means, in strict accuracy, Norfolk and Suffolk only, the
North-folk and the South-folk of the East Angles ; Essex
was the home of the East Saxons. However, this looseness
of terminology is scarcely matter for surprise when the
subject is a part of the country so habitually overlooked by
nearly all save those who live there, or have some close
connexion. For those who go for holidays at the watering-
places along the East Coast do not often pay much heed to
what is inland.

Thanks to geographical position, physical conditions
and the former close relations with the Low Countries, the
Eastern Counties exhibit strongly individual local traits
amongst the people and in the architecture of the churches,
towns and villages. In all likelihood, the architectural
development owes less to Flemish influence than is usually
imagined, but that does not greatly matter. Waves of
industrial development came in the fifteenth and seventeenth centuries when there was a vigorous tradition of
sound building, and there has almost always been a school
of fine craftsmanship preserving a character of restraint,

occasionally even of austerity, in marked contrast to the opulent elaboration prevailing in the south-western counties.

All three counties are practically destitute of stone ; the stone used for the churches and great houses had to be carried by sea or from stone-bearing counties. The typical village of the Eastern Counties is composed of timber houses, plastered or parged, and often coloured with light cream, rose, salmon or green washes. The domestic brickwork, too, in many places is of exceptionally pleasant quality ; this is notably the case in Norfolk. While the smaller churches in Essex are often of a type found in the southern counties, many of them, nevertheless, have timber belfries of a distinctive type. In Norfolk and Suffolk, thanks to the wealth derived from the mediæval cloth industry, there are many great churches filled with examples of splendid craftsmanship in carved wood, painted screens, and beautifully carved stalls. The East Anglian churches are noted, too, for their richly carved and sometimes polychrome oak roofs. Another characteristic frequently met with is an effective exterior use of flintwork, patterned with a variety of devices.

East Anglia is emphatically the land of mills—windmills (Plate xxxiii) on little knolls—post or tower mills, some few with sails still turning, especially if they are drainage mills in the fenland. Then there are watermills (Plate xxxv), great weather-boarded erections of many stories, towering up by the side of stream or pond, always with a little overhanging central piece to cover the tackle to hoist or lower the sacks.

None of the three counties, it is true, can lay claim to bold or hilly scenery such as you will find on the Welsh Borderland, in the Cotswolds or in the Berkshire Downs and the Chilterns, but in not a few places there are hills by no means contemptible, to say nothing of much pleasantly undulating country of a quiet pastoral type. Moreover, there are tracts of fen country (Plate xxxiv) reminiscent of Holland ; there are broad stretches of heath ; and, not least of all in their attraction, there are the Norfolk Broads (Plate xxxiii), a series of meres connected by winding, sluggish rivers, affording a natural feature not met with elsewhere. Likewise, there are the long reaches of chalk cliffs that occur at intervals along the coast. In short, there is a wide variety in the face of the land.

And there is scarcely a place that is not in some way connected with events of historic significance, or with notable persons. Even so apparently unimportant a hamlet as tiny Hempstead, on the northern boundary of Essex, has its cherished memories of Dick Turpin. At the little Rose and Crown Inn they will shew you the knot-hole in the floor boards of the bedchamber above the tap-room to which the youthful Dick used to glue his ear, when supposed to be asleep, and hearken to the gossip of daring highway robberies that fired his imagination and influenced all his after life. They will shew you, too, just across the road, the place where he used to hold his cock-fights, now marked by a ring of pollard willows. This same hamlet of Hempstead was also the birthplace of another celebrity, Dr. William Harvey, who discovered the circulation of the blood.

The fallacy of Essex flatness, like most fallacies, dies hard. It will probably never be eradicated, though it is unfounded, for Essex is definitely flat only round the seaboard. It is actually the hilliest of the three Eastern Counties.

Amongst the rolling chalk hills in the north-west, near Saffron Walden, the land often rises to more than four hundred feet. There are also other isolated quite hilly spots and, though perhaps it ought not to be told in Gath, the up Ipswich express has been known to be hung up on the grades round Brentwood till extra engine assistance arrived.

If Essex has been unfortunate in its reputation of un-deserved reproach, full justice has been done to its charm in Mr. Reginald Beckett's *Romantic Essex* and C. R. B. Barrett's two volumes, *Essex, Highways, Byways and Water-ways*. In the series of four volumes issued by the Royal Commission on Historical Monuments you will find abun-dant testimony to the wealth and beauty of its churches and houses.

In leaving London, avoid the high roads if possible ; in any event, haste to get away from them. The east and north-east districts, going out of London, are squalid, but

Epping Forest, save along its southern edge, remains sylvan, and the country to the south of it, by Abridge, is still surprisingly rural. Beyond Ongar you come to the Roding country, pastoral, quiet and unfrequented and, needless to say, little-known. Here the River Roding gives name to a whole cluster of villages—Beauchamp Roding, Margaret Roding, Berners Roding, Abbess Roding, White Roding, Aythorp Roding and High Roding (Plate xxxv). There may possibly be some more Rodings ; they seem to spread over the map and multiply like artichokes. Then, nearby, there are two other hamlet clusters, the Easters and the Lavers, to say nothing of Shellow Bowells, and Willingale Spain and Willingale Doe, with two churches in one churchyard.

The farm buildings of Essex are usually well-built and of large capacity, especially of the great barns constructed before the days of agricultural depression for the "tall Essex wheat" which used to cover many acres in this county renowned for its corn. A typical one of these from this district has been furnished by the Historical Monuments Commission.

To give any definite itinerary through this pleasant country would be a task both difficult and unduly long because, even within a restricted area, there are many places that it would be ungracious and wrong to omit.

There are so many spots of unexpected interest. Think of finding as you go along an old flint barn containing some of the actual remains of Saint Peter's-on-the-Wall, the original cathedral of Saint Chad, the apostle of East Anglia, It is just beyond Bradwell. Then, again, manor houses and other buildings of the Tudor period are plentiful in Essex, and indeed throughout all the Eastern Counties, and almost always in an appropriate setting (Fig. 22). Often you will chance upon them in the midst of a tangle of by-lanes, as at Layer Marney or Tolleshunt D'Arcy. Nor would you be wise to pass rapidly through such townlets as Coggeshall, Witham, Kelvedon or Maldon ; they abound in treasures. The places themselves are more or less familiar to people hastening through who know them only as names ; the treasures they hold are not well-known. You could never

ON THE RIVER YARE, NORFOLK

Painted by Edward Duncan, R.W.S.

PLATE XXXIV.

PLATE XXXV.

NEW HALL BARN, HIGH RODING

THE MILL, LANGHAM, ESSEX

count it a barren day, for example, if you had let your vagrant faring bring you to Laindon with its splendid timber-spired church and its hill whence, from an height of three hundred and fifty feet, you had gained a view of the Thames estuary and its world shipping.

Should you turn to the western side of the county, no river valley could offer more gentle, mellow beauty than that of the Pant from Braintree to Saffron Walden; no valley

Fig. 22.—Parham Old Hall, Suffolk.

Drawn by Sydney R. Jones.

could be more typical of the Eastern Counties. And yet the very name of the River Pant is but little known; it might be nearer the truth to say that it is almost unknown. The villages studding the sides of the Pant Valley—Pantfield, Wethersfield, Finchingfield, and the Sampfords—are altogether lovely.

At Finchingfield you will find such a village green as will long linger in your memory, a village green (Plate XXXVI) lying tilted up on the side of a hill, the stream and a duckpond at the bottom, houses rambling up along the sides, and the manor house set behind its trees and hedges at the top. Furthermore, you come upon this green as a surprise. Making your way through the closely built-up portion of the village, you pass the Norman church and the ancient alms-houses, turn a bend and plunge down a sharp little hill and you come to the stream and pond almost before you know it. There is a substantial stone bridge for vehicles to cross and a foot-bridge lower down at the end of the pond for dwellers on that side of the green. Before the ordinary, its sign of *The Green Man* is displayed from an iron frame splendidly wrought by some local smith of the old order of Craftsmanship. The timber and plaster houses, with thatch or red tile roofs, walls whitewashed or salmon-coloured or pale buff, have little gardens in front of them which in summer are filled with a fine display of flowers.

In Essex, too, as well as in the southern part of Suffolk and in Cambridgeshire, you will find many plastered outer walls enriched with pargetted patterns of all sorts. Some of this parge decoration is the simplest possible, consisting merely of wavy bands of parallel lines made with the teeth of a big wooden comb while the plaster is still moist. Again the patterns will be an elaborate arrangement of flowers, fruits and leafage, or will even include heraldic bearings, animals and human figures. You will see admirable examples of pargetting at Saffron Walden, Wivenhoe, Newport and Great Chesterford, and in a number of other places.

On your way to Braintree from the Rodings and the Easters and Lavers you have passed near Great and Little Dunmow, or perhaps you have taken a by-way and come through Little Dunmow. Great Dunmow is too much in evidence on a main highway to claim attention amongst little-known places, but Little Dunmow is out of the way and known, for the most part, only by the fame of the Dunmow Flitch. It is a pleasant village in exceeding pleasant country and has a parish church in which are incorporated portions of a once magnificent priory church destroyed at the time of the Dissolution. Here too, in the church are the alabaster effigies of Walter and Matilda Fitzwalter and here was buried their descendant Robert

Fitzwalter, a knight of King John's time, who not only is commonly credited with founding the custom of the Flitch of Bacon but also is known to have played his part in winning the Great Charter from his obdurate monarch. Stow tells us, of this same Robert Fitzwalter, how

"there arose great discord between King John and his barons, because of Matilda, surnamed the Fair, daughter to the said Robert Fitzwater, whom the King unlawfully loved, but could not obtain her, nor her father would consent, thereunto, whereupon, and for other like causes, ensued war through the whole realm. The barons were received into London where they greatly endamaged the King ; but in the end the King did not only therefore banish the said Fitzwater, amongst other, out of the realm, but also caused his castle called Baynard, and other his houses, to be spoiled ; which being done, a messenger being sent unto Matilda the Fair about the King's suit, whereunto she would not consent, she was poisoned ; Robert Fitzwater and other being then passed into France . . . . It happened in the year 1214, King John being then in France with a great army, that a truce was taken betwixt the two Kings of England and France for the term of five years ; and a river, or arm of the sea, being then between either host, there was a knight in the English host that cried to them of the other side willing some one of their knights to come and joust a course or twain with him : whereupon, without stay, Robert Fitzwater, being on the French part, made himself ready, ferried over, and got on horseback, without any man to help him, and shewed himself ready to the face of his challenger, whom at the first course he struck so hard with his great spear that horse and man fell to the ground ; and when his spear was broken he went back to the King of France ; which, when the King has seen, ' By God's troth ! ' quoth he (after his usual oath), ' he were a King indeed that had such a knight.' The friends of Robert, hearing these words, kneeled down and said, ' O King, he is your knight, it is Robert Fitzwater.' And thereupon the next day he was sent for, and restored to the King's favour, by which means peace was concluded, and he received his livings, and had licence to repair his castle of Baynard, and other castles."

As leader of the rebellious barons, Fitzwalter was styled Marshall of the Army of God and of Holy Church.

It affords an interesting sidelight upon Fitzwalter's

personality to find him instituting upon his Manor of Little Dunmow a custom intended to set a premium upon conjugal felicity. The flitch was given at the joint charge of the prior and his canons and of the lord of the manor; it was awarded to applicant couples who took their oath, kneeling on two sharp stones in the churchyard, that they had neither quarrelled nor repented their marriage for a year and a day. Then followed a general village festivity. After the Dissolution the Dunmow Flitch was awarded on several occasions, but the custom was brought definitely to an end late in the eighteenth century. The modern revival started by Harrison Ainsworth smacks of bank holiday farce. The so-called "Bacon Chair" is to be seen in the sacristy, but this was probably the Prior's seat in the refectory which was rescued on the destruction of the priory. It seems anomalous that there is no worthy monument to Robert Fitzwalter, certainly the greatest man that Essex produced in the Middle Ages if not, indeed, the greatest Englishman of the period.

Thaxted (Plate xxxvi), though a sizeable town, is curiously enough but little-known, little-known even for Essex, and yet Thaxted was an important place in its day and the traces of its glory are still visible. Thaxted means the " thatched place " and a reminder of this once universal roofing you will find hung under the floor joists of the upper storey of the Moot Hall (Plate xxxvii) in the shape of two long poles, with iron hooks attached, that were used in bygone days for pulling the burning thatch from houses a-fire. In the Middle Ages, before coal had supplanted wood as fuel, Thaxted was the Sheffield of England and was famous for its cutlery. The memory of Thaxted's makers of knives and swords is perpetuated in the name of an adjacent hamlet, Cutlers' Green.

As you come into the town from the south there is a broad street, the houses on both sides of which offer many an engaging theme in domestic architecture. Anon the street divides. To the right you go up hill past the inns and the north side of the church; to the left there is a broad passage past another row of beguiling houses, both brick and timbered with overhanging upper storeys, and leading

PLATE XXXVI.

FINCHINGFIELD, ESSEX

THE ENTRANCE TO THAXTED

PLATE XXXVII.

THE CHURCH FROM GOLD STREET, SAFFRON WALDEN

THE GUILD HALL, THAXTED, ESSEX

BEFORE THE REMOVAL OF THE PLASTER PANELS

to the churchyard and the south side of the church. At the point of the Y stands the mediæval Moot Hall upborne by sturdy oaken columns, an open arcade beneath with an overhanging storey above. Nearby is a little house called Dick Turpin's house, which seems to have figured in some episode of his career.

The chief glory of Thaxted is its splendid church which has been called, not inappropriately, the Cathedral of Essex. Its great size and loftiness bear witness to the wealth and numbers of a mediæval trading community and the generosity of a noble patron, in this case no less a person than Edward IV. The size and beauty of the churches, here and elsewhere, bear witness to something else that we ought not to overlook, something that accounts for an inherited local pride in old churches throughout England on the part of townspeople and villagers even amongst chapel folk. Before the Reformation church buildings had a distinct manifold secular function as well as an ecclesiastical function; the two were interwoven and people lived their religion daily. When the Rev. J. E. Vaux writes, in *Church Folklore* " the naves of our cathedrals and parish churches seem to have been regarded as the common homes of the people," he is not at all overstating the case.

"From the Englishman's cradle, the first thought of his parents was his baptism in the parish church, and the public churching of his mother. His approaching marriage was announced by banns being called in his parish church, as well as in that of his bride. The ceremony was celebrated by the joyous pealing of the church bells. The church's festivals were his own holidays. The announcement of his death was conveyed to the parish and his neighbours by a solemn knell from the church tower. To be buried in the graveyard of his fathers was his last desire. Here collections for the poor were made, and public notices affixed to the doors . . . . The principal porch was the place of village assembly, and frequently the place of record for legal arrangements, judgments given, deeds signed. Over the porch the chamber was occupied by a school or by a library. The south porch was frequently used for housing vagrants ; indeed every parishioner had the right to make it a shelter for the night in case of necessity. We have even records of women in childbirth being allowed to occupy the south porch. A hundred illustrations could be given of the relation of the church to the parish. But the most important of all was that it stood the tangible source of moral instruction in every town and village. Seeing all this, how great is the value of these ancient buildings as historic monuments! The intense interest felt in the architectural beauty of many of them simply pales before the sentiments aroused by a consideration of their human interest. The home of the national faith and morals for upwards of a thousand years—that is the parish church in England."

Through high gently rolling country, you come to Saffron Walden (Plate xxxvii), another town with a magnificent Perpendicular church of great size. Saffron Walden got the first of its names in the time of Edward III from the extensive cultivation of the saffron crocus in the neighbourhood. Before that time it was simply Walden, the "town in the woods," or Chipping Walden to denote that a market was held there. The saffron plant, the original bulbs of which were brought, so it is said, by a palmer from the Holy Land, is no longer grown.

Saffron Walden is filled with good domestic architecture for the delight of those who have leanings that way, both houses of Georgian parentage and dwellings of earlier type, timbered, plastered and shewing much excellent parge decoration. It also has its full complement of old inns, if you have a fancy for "collecting" old inns, and inn-collecting, be assured is a more many-sided and fascinating hobby than might at first be imagined. The Sun Inn, now much restored and occupied as a dwelling, once sheltered Oliver Cromwell, if we may credit local tradition, but there are plenty more to let the inn "collector" satisfy his bent. One of them, the Rose and Crown, he will surely want for his "bag." Though re-fronted with brick in 1690, "new sashed and beautified in the year 1748," and kept nowadays in the pink of perfection, there is a great deal of the original Tudor work remaining. Besides that, the Rose and Crown is something of a literary shrine for, in 1609, the landlord was one J. Holgate and his son, young William Holgate, a poet himself and the associate of literary men, seems to have been the mysterious " Mr. W. H." to whom Shakespeare dedicated his Sonnets.

If you choose to spend some time poking about Saffron Walden, you will probably unearth many a strange or diverting thing. You may even come upon the trail of the " Flying Serpent " which a rare old tract, printed about 1669, tells of as having been seen in earlier days at Henham-on-the-Mount, near Saffron Walden. The monster wrought much havoc, but " a valiant knight made a ' Coat of Christel Glass ' so pure that the cockatrice expired at the sight of it. The sword of the knight was hung up in Walden Church, and his effigies set up in brass there, near which a ' table hanged wherein was contained all the story of the adventure.' " During the Rebellion, the Cromwellians regarded all this as grossly superstitious and destroyed all the documentary evidence of the monster's existence and the knight's prowess.

Taking your way out of Saffron Walden towards the east, after six or seven miles you come to the hamlet of Hempstead, Dick Turpin's and Doctor Harvey's birthplace, as you have already learned. The road brings you very soon to Steeple Bumpstead, a pretty little village with some fascinating old houses and a stream, named apparently on the " lucus a non lucendo " principle, for the church has only a tower and not the least vestige of a steeple. The Wesleyan chapel, it seems, taking the inconsistency to heart has tried to remedy the shortcoming by displaying the sharpest and spikiest of steeplets. After a water-splash at Helion Bumpstead the same road lands you in a short time at the Upper Stour Valley and the southern edge of Suffolk.

Suffolk is just as hard to summarise as is its southern neighbour, for the face of the land is just as varied, though perhaps the contrasts are not so sharp. Again there are just as wide differences between the villages, and you will find certain little local diversities amongst the people themselves. It may not have the dramatic quality to be met with in some other counties but it possesses in rich measure a subtle, soft beauty.

You enter Clare (Plate xxxviii) by a broad street where

more than one decorous Georgian house front is belied by moulded brick chimney stacks rising above the roofs only half-concealed by the Classic parapet. In the eighteenth century, Clare wished to be comely and in the fashion. To be comely then, meant to disguise timbered walls or Tudor brickwork with an exterior jacket of Classic mould; to be comely now means to eschew the futilities of commercialised technique and materials. Then it was *de rigueur* to obliterate the appearance of age; now it is *de rigueur* to preserve it. Clare, fortunately for the lover of unspoiled country towns, has kept its eighteenth century aspects unmarred and, at the same time, has retained not a few of its earlier timbered buildings or parged fronts.

Turning north from Clare, you soon find yourself at Poslingford; in spite of a messed up church it is a village of agreeable presence with a lovely approach, a water-splash and a bridge. Climbing a ridge and turning east before reaching Stansfield, a detour—part of the way through lanes so twisted and involved that they seem to have been devised by a serpent in pain—takes you past Thurston End, a typical Suffolk manor house of Tudor days, to Swans Hall, now a farm, a perfect and more un-spoiled Tudor house, timbered with herringbone brickwork.

Going back past Thurston End, a steep road to the right plunges down into a wooded valley, crosses the infant Glem and mounts another hill to Hawkeden, its church in the middle of the green and a duck pond in one corner, the cottages standing at a distance around the borders of this open upland as though waiting expectantly to see what the church and the duck pond would do if left to themselves. Thence a short stretch lands you at the village green of Hartest, another of those almost unbelievable places that seem to have stepped bodily from the pages of an old story-book or to have been cleverly contrived as a piece of stage setting. The old houses bordering the green (Plate xxxviii) are pleasant enough in every way, but it is the *ensemble* that creates the spell—houses marked by the divers characteristics of placid village life; the broad green of irregular shape sloping gently down towards the far corner where a lane leads off from the church closely embowered

PLATE XXXVIII.

THE MARKET PLACE, CLARE, SUFFOLK

A CORNER OF THE VILLAGE GREEN, HARTEST

ST. JAMES'S CHURCH AND "SIX BELLS" INN, BURY ST. EDMUND

Painted by Michael Angelo Rooker, A.R.A.

PLATE XXXIX.

in great trees ; the oaks and the elms growing near the ends
of the open area ; and the vistas of the meadows beyond
where cattle graze and the stream runs beneath willows and
alders. Though the picture is not ineffective, no lens, as
at Finchingfield, can do justice to the wide extent and varied
features of the village.

Through a succession of typical villages you come to
Bury Saint Edmunds, one of the few places in East Anglia
that most people seem to know at all, and Bury Saint
Edmunds is none too well known. You could easily
devote a day merely to seeing the " sights "—the Adam
Town Hall, the Norman bell-tower of the vanished Abbey,
one of the greatest in England, and the splendid fifteenth
century churches, Saint Mary's and Saint James's, the
latter now the Cathedral of the new diocese (Plate xxxix).
Bury was " famed for its pleasant situation and wholesome
air," as Daniel Defoe wrote early in the eighteenth century,
" the Montpellier of Suffolk, and perhaps of England."
Defoe lived for a time at Bury and evidently enjoyed his
residence there ; and he wrote of it, the town was
" crowded with nobility and gentry, and all sorts of the most
agreeable company ; and as the company invites, so there is
the appearance of pleasure upon the very situation ; and
they that live at Bury are supposed to live there for the sake
of it." Elsewhere he adds," the beauty of this town con-
sists in the number of gentry who dwell in and near it, the
polite conversation among them, the affluence and plenty
they live in, the sweet air they breathe in, and the pleasant
country they have to go abroad in." More than a century
after Defoe, another keen observer was equally impressed
with the town's social poise and self-sufficiency as a " little
metropolis of the squirearchy, where the dowagers retired
for life into the family mansions . . . . . There was no
lord in the place to adorn it, but there was a great plenty
of the kind to bless it and conserve it within reach."

Bury's praises, as a goodly place to dwell, were sung
likewise by John Leland early in the sixteenth century.

" City more neatly seated," he wrote, " the sun never saw,
so curiously doth it hang upon a gentle descent, with a little
river upon the east side (the Lark) ; nor a monastery more

99

noble, whether one considers its endowments, largeness, or unparalleled magnificence. One might even think the monastery alone a city; so many gates it has (some whereof are brass), so many towers, and a church, than which nothing can be more magnificent; as appendages to which, there are three more of admirable beauty and workmanship in the same churchyard."

A disaster in 1608 greatly changed the face of the town. Stow records that on April 11 of that year

" . . . being Monday, the Quarter Sessions was held at St. Edmondsbury, and by Negligence an Out-Malthouse was set on fire; from whence in most strange and sudden manner, through fierce Winds, the Fire came to the farthest side of the Town, and as it went, left some Streets and Houses safe and untouched. The flames flew clean over many Houses near it, and did great spoil to many fair Buildings farthest off; and ceased not till it had consumed One hundred and sixty Dwelling-Houses, besides others; and in Damage of Wares and Household-stuff to the full Value of Sixty Thousand Pounds."

East and North from Bury our road passes through Great Barton, Pakenham, Stowlangtoft, where there is an excellent specimen of the old East Anglian post windmill, Hunston, with some particularly fascinating old farmhouses, and so to Walsham-le-Willows; thence, bearing due north, you are headed for the Norfolk boundary and a bit of heath country, first running through Barningham and its cluster of thatched cottages and Coney Weston. The solitary track is hemmed in on both sides by thick screens of high, uncut hedgerow, trees, and unpruned thorns that have grown into trees; now and again, startled from the wonted quiet of this unfrequented way, coneys, pheasants and partridges dart across before you. Just before crossing the border, in an especially lonely neighbourhood, you come to the deserted little fourteenth century church of Knettishall, smothered in ivy, left to bats and owls, the churchyard overgrown with briars and brambles, the sole relic of what was once a community.

Almost immediately beyond Knettishall church you cross the Norfolk boundary and pass the hamlet of Gasthorpe, consisting of only a few thatched cottages. The River

Waveney separates the counties, and a few miles further down its course, on the main London-Norwich road, is the village of Scole (Fig. 23), with the excellent White Hart Inn of 17th century brickwork. Then your way takes you across Garboldisham Heath and East Harling Heath, the Devil's Ditch at your right side and the heathland (Plate XL) all around, a particularly lonely bit of country. Garboldisham Heath is a broad expanse of general parklike

Fig. 23.—The Yard of the " White Hart," Scole.

Drawn by A. H. Mottram.

character, dotted with clumps of gorse, patches of bracken and scattered groups of beech and pine trees. The road is unfenced and so continues much of the distance to East Harling, a small market town with a fine old church whose rood screen is enriched with mediæval polychrome panels.

Not far ahead is Attleborough, strung out along the highway, and beyond lies Wymondham, one of the gems of Norfolk. The old timbered Moot Hall and the ancient houses of Wymondham invite you to dally and explore the place at leisure, and such time you would find well spent, but the chiefest treasure is the church, a noble structure originally Norman which, large as it is, is but half the original structure. This glorious building has a tower at each end; the tower at the west end is intact and contains the parish peal of bells. The octagonal tower at the east end is ruinous; this was the central tower of the abbey church (Fig. 24) and east of it the conventual church was

Fig. 24.—Wymondham Church from the South-west.

Drawn by W. Curtis Green, A.R.A.

of like extent with the nave, now the parish church, at the west. At the Dissolution all the monastic buildings, including the eastern half of the abbey church, were allowed to go to ruin, leaving only the half-ruinous central tower and the west limb, with its own tower, to continue as the parish church. The Norman nave dates from about 1107. The arrangement by which the parishioners had the use of the monastic nave dated from 1349, so the placing of the chancel in the last bay of the nave building has been con-

PLATE XL.

THE "DOG AND PARTRIDGE," LOOKING TO ST. MARY'S,
BURY ST. EDMUNDS

ON A NORFOLK HEATH
THE PEDLAR'S WAY, NEAR THOMPSON

PLATE XLI.

THE RIVER OUSE AND BRIDGE, BRANDON

OXBURGH HALL AND MOAT, NORFOLK

tinuous for nearly six centuries. The monastic crossing
and sanctuary were shut off by a mighty stone screen.
Protracted disputes between the monks and the townsfolk
about ringing the bells in the Central Tower determined the
parishioners to build their own tower; hence the stately
structure at the west end, dating from 1445-76. Nothing
could be more splendidly dramatic than the sight of
Wymondham Church, as you enter the churchyard from the
north-east late in the afternoon of a grey November day, the
double avenue of Scotch firs pointing gaunt fingers towards
the ruined tower.

From Wymondham a few miles will bring you into
Hingham, the parent of the Massachusetts town of like
name. A seventeenth century rector of Hingham in
Norfolk, being a somewhat cantankerous personage and
having got into trouble with the ecclesiastical authorities,
gathered a band of sympathetic fellow townsmen, crossed
the Atlantic and planted Hingham in Massachusetts. His
contentiousness there seems to have caused unpleasant
feeling and he subsequently came back to England to be
more or less of a storm centre of agitation till his death.

Hingham is doubtless an agreeable place in pleasant
weather, but it was certainly gaunt and bleak when the
writer arrived there for the first time on a raw Sunday
evening in March, and the natural conditions were un-
doubtedly heightened by an unfavourable experience at
one of the inns, about which the less said the better. It
is well to bear in mind that the accommodation in small
places is limited, and unless arrangements have been made
beforehand, the arrival should be timed so that it is possible
to go further should quarters not be available. Fortunately
the writer was able to secure comfortable private sleeping
quarters, which can usually be obtained as the result of a
few careful, persistent inquiries, and on this particular
occasion he counted himself fortunate to discover the
modest little Cock Inn, where, although sickness in the
house precluded the provision of accommodation, there was
a hospitable welcome and excellent homely, satisfying meals.

Apart from this unhappy instance, a case of distinct in-
hospitality at North Walsham, and the grim behaviour of

a barmaid in Great Yarmouth, who went into a tantrum on being asked to supply a rum toddy on a cold morning, the writer has always met the utmost cordiality in Norfolk, and there are numerous places which it is a genuine pleasure to enter. At The Globe at King's Lynn, for instance, you are made to feel thoroughly welcome; it is one of those places where you know they are going to put a hot-water bottle in your bed without being told, and where you always experience a hundred and one little unasked-for attentions that indicate the prevailing spirit of thoughtful kindliness.

In view of the connection between the two sides, it is possible that the rather nonchalant indifference sometimes to be found in Norfolk and New England is derived from a characteristic in the racial stock. There is occasionally detected in some parts of New England a somewhat " go-and-hang-yourself" attitude in certain strata of the population.

Hingham lies in the midst of a quiet pastoral district without any particular scenic features, but there are many interesting places around. At Deopham Church is a splendid mighty Perpendicular west tower with patterned flintwork. Morley St. Botolph has one of the un-aisled churches with a long nave, a characteristic occasionally found locally, and across the railway at Barnham Broom is one of Norfolk's characteristic old brick halls with a fine modelled plaster ceiling. Further to the west lies Scoulton with its mere, which is the haunt of hundreds of wild fowl. At Holme Hale are some fine poppy heads; Necton has a most magnificent and individual roof. Hardingham, mentioned later, has a curious little church, of which the tower forms the south porch. The rector who was dispossessed during the Commonwealth lingered on in the village, and when his little daughter died he took one of the flint squares out of a buttress on the south side and cut with his own hands her little epitaph, "Mary Joscelyne sleepeth," a pathetic touch of fatherly affection.

From Hingham you can readily either strike off north-westward through Swaffham and across the heath towards King's Lynn, Castle Rising and Hunstanton, or else you can hold a generally northward course through East Dereham, Fakenham and the Walsinghams to Wells-next-the-Sea.

Supposing you do the former, you will find Swaffham an agreeable town with its houses chiefly ranged about a spacious market place, an exceedingly graceful butter cross whose domical roof is upborne by eight stone columns, and a noble fifteenth century parish church—restored and enlarged at that time—whose chief pride is its wonderful double-hammer-beam roof with some two hundred angels carved thereon. The glorious carved roofs are one of the noted peculiarities of East Anglian churches, and the roof of Swaffham Church holds a conspicuous place amongst the best. There is a curious old legend connected with the rebuilding of Swaffham Church that runs as follows :—

A Swaffham pedlar, one John Chapman, "dreamed that if he went to London and stood on London Bridge he would there meet with a man who would tell him joyful news. Three times he had the same dream, and then he determined to go to London and see whether it would come true. Arrived at London town, he took his stand on the Bridge, when he was questioned by a man who had noticed him aimlessly waiting there hour after hour.

The pedlar told his story, and the man was surprised that anyone should be such a fool as to act on a silly dream. 'I'll tell thee, country fellow,' he added, 'that last night I dreamed I was at Swaffham, in Norfolk, a place unknown to me, where methought if I digged behind a pedlar's house under a great oak tree I should find vast treasure. If I should have made a journey thither to dig for such hidden treasure, judge you whether I should not have been counted a fool.'

The pedlar, on hearing this, declared that he would go home and never heed such dreams again, but as soon as he reached Swaffham he began to dig under the oak tree behind his house and eventually found a great pot full of money. After carefully concealing the coin he placed the empty pot among his brass ware, but a caller at the house pointed out an inscription on the pot in Latin, which the pedlar had not noticed. In English it read :

"Under me doth lie
Another far richer than I."

The pedlar said that this was true, for when he bought the pot, another stood under it twice the size. The words of the inscription, however, stimulated the pedlar to dig still deeper, and he was rewarded by finding a larger pot with greater treasure. One of the first deeds after the acquisition of these unexpected riches was to restore Swaffham Church, which had fallen into a ruinous condition, and there, to this day, on a prayer desk in the chancel, are the carved oak effigies of the pedlar and his muzzled dog."

A picturesque bit, the probably apocryphal tale, but it helps you to remember Swaffham.

Swaffham is at the north-eastern edge of the strangely individual heath country which stretches southward all the way to the Suffolk border at Brandon (Plate XLI) and Thetford. In this district of rolling heathland are several fine Tudor halls of brick or terracotta—Great Cressingham Priory, Methwold Rectory and the moated pile at Oxburgh (Plate XLI), with one of the great tower gatehouses, such as are seen at Layer Marney and Hadleigh deanery.

From Swaffham across the heath it is not a long run to King's Lynn, and to be in the neighbourhood of King's Lynn and not go there would be little short of a crime; then, too, the drive over the heath with its pines and bracken will give you an insight into some of the variety of country that Norfolk can boast. King's Lynn, lying on the Ouse just where it joins the Wash, is one of the most self-possessed, most self-contained old towns you could possibly imagine. Its whole air plainly shews that it is conscious of its great past, that it has its own worthy traditions, and that it cares not a straw how the world wags. For centuries it was one of the greatest of the eastern sea-port towns, did a thriving trade with the Hanseatic League, and was the port through which most of the wine brought from abroad entered England.

One of the most charming small civil buildings in the kingdom is the Customs House (Fig. 25), built in the latter part of the seventeenth century and designed by Henry Bell, a Lynn architect of great ability. It is impossible to go into the Tuesday Market (Plate XLII)—the market square on which The Globe's dining-room windows look out—without both regret and indignation that, in 1839, a "committee of taste" was responsible for demolishing Bell's Market Cross, a structure of not less distinction than

PLATE XLII.

TUESDAY MARKET PLACE, KING'S LYNN, 1797
(FROM AN OLD PRINT)

WIGGENHALL ST. GERMANS, NORFOLK

PLATE XLIII.

OLD HUNSTANTON, NORFOLK

BLAKENEY, NORFOLK
THE CHURCH WITH ITS MEDIAEVAL LIGHTHOUSE

the Customs House; we have only old sketches and engravings of it left. Then there is Saint Margaret's Church, one of the most splendid parish churches in England, with abundant wealth of history attached to it; and there is the Church of Saint Nicholas, a noble pile, and really a chapel of ease to the mother parish; there is likewise the Guild Hall, a well-preserved flint chequer building filled with all manner of treasures, not the least of which is the famous King John Cup; and there is the Greenland Fishery house, now a museum containing all sorts of

Fig. 25.—The Customs House, King's Lynn.

Drawn by Sydney R. Jones.

wonderful things connected with Lynn's past glory. Incidentally, it is very easy from Lynn to explore the fen country, to run to Wisbech and fancy, when you get there, that you have suddenly dropped into a Dutch town with a river or a canal for the High Street; to go along to Castle Rising with its alluring ruins and its hospital full of red-coated pensioners; or to continue to Hunstanton and on along the north coast. Around King's Lynn is the splendid group of stately marshland churches, which Norfolk shares with Cambridgeshire and Lincolnshire; the Terringtons, the Tilneys, the Walpoles, Walsoken, West Walton, and the Wiggenhalls. These latter, including little St. Germans by the river (Plate XLII), are full of splendid benches. Old Hunstanton (Plate XLIII), another typical village, affords a strong contrast to the little hamlet on the Ouse.

Leaving Hingham to the north you can pass Hardingham Church, the parish church for several little scattered hamlets with the church and rectory quite isolated like a sun in the midst of its constellation. Near by Hardingham Church is Old Hall Farm, a late seventeenth brick house of excellent type.

Between holly edges, and beeches and oaks growing out of the hedges and making an almost continuous avenue of trees, the undulating lane carries you through Letton, Southburgh, and Cranworth to Shipdham (Fig. 26) with its strange wood and lead lanthorn atop the church; thence on to East Dereham, the central market town of Norfolk, a prepossessing place of chiefly Georgian aspect. In 1581, and again in 1670, the town suffered disastrous fires and Bonner's Cottages, built in 1502, a row of thatched roof dwellings with rich parge decorations on the fronts, appear to have been the only houses in the town that escaped both conflagrations.

Fig. 26.—The Lead Spire, Shipdham Church, Norfolk.

All the towns and villages between East Dereham and Wells-next-the-Sea have one feature or another to arrest attention and invite a stop, and the countryside is fair to look upon; but Fakenham, another tidy market town, East

Barsham, with its splendid brick ruined house of the Tudor period, and the Walsinghams, enshrouded in their memories of the great days of mediæval pilgrimages, are the most important. Wells-next-the-Sea will remind you in a way of King's Lynn. By no means so large, and without the great mercantile past that Lynn enjoyed, Wells nevertheless has enough of the same confident poise and self-sufficient bearing to cause the reminiscence, especially in the calm dignity of the houses facing the green. In summertime, bathing and sailing add to the attractions.

Turning east and south from Wells-next-the-Sea, a road that pretty closely parallels the curve of the coast takes you through Stiffkey, Blakeney and Cley, and thence across Salthouse Heath to Bessingham. At Blakeney you will be struck by the unusual appearance of the church (Plate XLIII) whose eastern towerlet, visible far out at sea, has been a beacon for centuries.

The church at Cley is one of the most beautiful in northern Norfolk and possesses a number of unusual features. The rich Decorated transept, abandoned unfinished at the Black Death and ruinous since, is now about to be restored— *really* restored and not messed about. Like not a few other places in East Anglia, Cley once had a far larger population than now, but the silting up of the harbour, and the increase in the size of ships, sealed Cley's fate as a port, and for generations past it has been a rural community. From Cley the road lies part of the way amidst the heather and bracken of Salthouse Heath, and from the open rolling downland hereabouts, thanks to its elevation of about two hundred feet, you can look out to sea ; sky and sea, heather and bracken, and the gentle swell of the downs combine to make a picture you will not soon forget.

Beyond the heath, the way carries you through pleasant farming country with occasional stretches of woodland. Not long after passing through Thorpe Market you come to Knapton, a not especially prepossessing village, but having a church whose double hammer-beam roof, polychromed and carved with an whole choir of flying angels, is one of the most splendid in all East Anglia (Plate XLIV), and when one knows East Anglian church roofs, that is saying much. It is a thing worth going miles out of the way to see. While you are in Knapton you are close to Paston, the village associated with the Paston family and the famous Paston Letters. Thence it is not far to North Walsham where you may take roads that run at times close enough to some of the Broads to give you occasional glimpses of their shining surfaces.

To reach Ranworth you can turn off the main road and take a ferry across the River Bure. Horning ferry is managed by a man and an Airedale terrier; the terrier gives notice of your arrival and the man comes out of the ferry house to take you across the water, all under the terrier's close supervision; if anyone comes from the other side, he rings a big bell to attract the ferryman's attention. The village of Ranworth is small, remote and picturesque in its wooded setting, but the real purpose of going there is to see the wonderful fifteenth-century painted rood-screen (Plate XLIV), intact in all its parts and in the rich colour of its figured panels and carven tracery. Ranworth Church is kept in good repair, it is comforting to know, but there was a time within the memory of people still living when it had fallen into such dilapidation that a donkey was found one day grazing on the grass growing between the floor stones of the aisles and the parson sometimes had to read service under the shelter of an umbrella.

After you leave the lovely country around Ranworth Broad, there is nothing to detain you in the immediate neighbourhood before reaching Great Yarmouth. At Fritton, on the road to Beccles, is a strange little thatched apsidal church (Plate XLV) with a round flint tower; though utterly simple, it is the sort of thing that fixes itself in the memory.

Southwold, over the border in Suffolk, is a sizeable town and somewhat by way of being a watering place. Nevertheless, parts of it possess genuine attraction for one who loves unspoiled England, and Southwold Church is an example of fifteenth century East Anglian flint architecture of the foremost rank, besides containing carved woodwork and other riches of great interest. You may note that there is a

PLATE XLIV.

KNAPTON CHURCH—THE NAVE ROOF

THE SCREEN, RANWORTH, NORFOLK

PLATE XLV.

FRITTON CHURCH, SUFFOLK

Drawn by H. Davy, 1826

LADY STREET, LAVENHAM

LOOKING TO WATER STREET AND THE OLD WOOL HALL. THE HALF TIMBER
GABLE ON THE EXTREME RIGHT HAS DISAPPEARED

tombstone near the churchyard gate to mark the grave of one Benjamin Lousey.

     *   *   *   *   *

When leaving Bury Saint Edmunds, if you had taken a road to the south, instead of going north-east you would have come in due time to Lavenham (Plate XLV), a village that has kept as much of its fifteenth century character as any place in England. It was once one of the great East Anglian cloth towns and most of it remains as it was when the streets resounded to the noise of the looms and the

Fig. 27.——Church Street, Lavenham.

Drawn by John S. Corder.

great clothiers amassed fortunes which they lavished on their magnificent church and their own houses. The church, mainly of the fifteenth century, contains some marvellous wood-carving in the screens enclosing the Spring and Branch chapels ; the splendour of the building is chiefly due to the munificence of John de Vere, thirteenth Earl of Oxford, and Thomas Spring, a wealthy Lavenham clothier, the third of his name.

Besides the church, however, the Guild Hall, the old Wool Hall, the ancient inns and many fifteenth and six-teenth century timbered dwellings (Fig. 27) retain their character unspoiled and give Lavenham an aspect most consistently complete. To America especially it is interesting to remember that the Winthrops, who figured so conspicuously in planting the New England Colonies in America, came from Lavenham and kept up for many years a close connexion with the village after their initial settlement across the Atlantic.

From Lavenham the countryside is unfailingly pleasant, and such villages as Brent Eleigh, Monk's Eleigh, Bildeston, Kersey and Stoke-by-Nayland repay you with many an unspoiled picture. Kersey and Stoke-by-Nayland are especially inviting. Kersey is one of the old cloth centres and the kind of cloth woven there was so famous for its distinctive quality that Kersey's name is known the world over; the village itself, its cloth prosperity now only a memory of the long-departed past, remains one of the gems of little-known England. As you enter the village by a winding street (Plate XLVI), drive through a water-splash and climb the steep hill towards the church, you will catch many glimpses that will carry you back to the fifteenth and sixteenth centuries. In the church you will find a beautiful hammer-beam roof supported by flying angels, with all their heads gone. For this wanton decapitation we have to thank the Cromwellian soldiers, who apparently had an universal spite against the heavenly host. The roof of the flint-patterned south porch, though gloriously carved and polychromed, has only foliated *motifs*, so that they " brake not this with axes and hammers." Stoke-by-Nayland, though quite different in every way from Kersey, is no less endowed with that compelling beauty which is often the quality of the small English village.

Whatever road you take in this part of Suffolk is certain to bring you to some place that will repay a visit. Such places, for example, are Sudbury (Plate XLVII) and its associations with Gainsborough, or Long Melford with its Tudor brick Hall, its church at the top of a long slope, and its cottages sprinkled about the edges of a spacious green. Of utterly different character is the grim old ruin of Castle Hedingham (Fig. 28, p. 128) not far away in Essex, once one of the most splendid Norman castles in

PLATE XLVI.

LOOKING SOUTH TO THE CHURCH

THE WATERSPLASH

LOOKING NORTH

KERSEY, SUFFOLK

WATER LANE, STRATFORD, SUFFOLK

Drawing by John Constable, R.A.

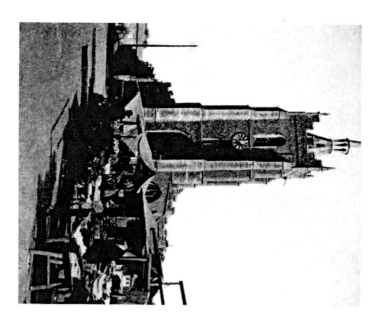

THE MARKET PLACE AND CHURCH, SUDBURY

PLATE XLVII.

England, the home of the de Veres, Earls of Oxford, who lived in it for more than five hundred years. Much of the ruin was wrought by Edward de Vere, the seventeenth Earl of Oxford, in the time of Queen Elizabeth of whose Court he was a brilliant member. When Thomas Howard, Duke of Norfolk—Edward de Vere's dearest friend—was under sentence of death, de Vere petitioned Robert Cecil, Lord Burleigh, to save the Duke's life. The petition was in vain and thereupon Edward de Vere took the following method of avenging his friend's death. Cecil's daughter Anne was the Earl's wife and Hedingham Castle was her jointure. The Earl repudiated his wife and set to work to wreck the castle, " disparked the parks, pulled down the outbuildings and cut down the timber." All this mischief turned out to be quite useless, for the unfortunate Anne died before her husband. Edward de Vere married again and " in digust would have sold Castle Hedingham had not his second wife by a kindly act continued to preserve the estate for the family."

At Sible Hedingham near by the tower is sculptured on its outer walls with flying hawks which seem to have something to do with the Hawkwood family and that bluff old warrior, Sir John de Hawkwood, of whom romantic tales are told. He fought under Edward III and, if tradition may be trusted, had a brilliant career as a *condottiere* in the incessant north Italian wars of the period.

On all the way back to London, there is scarcely a spot in Essex around which historic associations do not cluster; everywhere you find quiet, peaceful beauty of some diversity. If you set forth to see the little-known parts of England, it matters not at what season of the year, nor in which of the four regions to which this book is devoted, you will find recompenses incomparably rich and of a sort that will be ever afterwards a treasured possession.

CHAPTER V

OUTLINE SUMMARY OF THE FOUR DISTRICTS AND MAP SECTION

Practical Touring Hints—Shropshire—Herefordshire—The Cotswolds —The Chalk Hills—The Eastern Counties : Essex—Suffolk— Norfolk.

A FEW BRIEF PRACTICAL TOURING HINTS

ENGLAND is a pleasant country to tour and with some easily acquired *savoir faire* it is practicable to ramble inexpensively. The thronged highroads can, and should, be avoided, as most parts outside the northern moorlands are splendidly roaded, and by-roads and lanes have usually excellent surfaces. But avoid tracks of inferior surface, easily distinguised as uncoloured on the map ; practice will soon give the knack of distinguishing between the advantageous and the impracticable. Learn to work out your own itinerary with a map ; Bartholomew's coloured ½-inch to the mile is an excellent series for general touring ; a smaller scale is not usually advisable. But pedestrian strolls get right to the heart of the country, and for such intimate work the Ordnance 1-inch to the mile (large sheet series) is indispensable. Most districts are well signposted, but in lack of this guidance the people, though friendly, are sometimes not very helpful in direction and few English have the "map sense."

Unless your tastes are inclined in that direction, there is no need to patronise elaborate and expensive large hotels in towns ; many less pretentious places offer equal or better fare at more moderate figures ; for guides there are the Automobile and other motoring Association handbooks, and the Michelin Series, that of the Cyclists' Touring Club, and the Kuklos Annual ("Daily News Office"). The vigorous and youthful can hire reliable bicycles, or for an extended tour buy a second-hand pedal or motor-cycle ; in the latter case an expert inspection is advisable. The vehicle can then be sold for a fair price at the conclusion of the trip ; the same procedure is also applied to a motor car with successful results. Since the war all towns have a number of helpful motor omnibus services running out to various villages and through to cities and other towns. To the non-motorist these are of extreme value, and timetables, giving omnibus and local rail services can usually be had for a few pence at station bookstalls and stationers' shops. Recently through motor coach services have been established between all great towns, and a splendid full programme of both motor coaches and nearly all motor omnibus services is issued monthly by Roadways Time Tables, Ltd. ; its value is beyond words. If any difficulty is found in obtaining it, write to the firm at Regency House, Warwick Street, London, W.1.

For those who prefer it, private lodgings can usually be obtained by reference to a policeman or small post-office ; they are often inexpensive and offer some advantages. Farmhouses are usually attractive as centres for exploration ; lists of private country lodgings are compiled in some of the guides already mentioned, and in the annual Holiday Handbooks issued cheaply by the great railway companies— L.M.S., L.N.E.R., G.W.R., and S.R. But give some notice in a village or small town ; most catering folk dread being " taken unawares " and in small places resources of all kinds are naturally limited.

The English country inn whether in village or small town is fairly often ill-equipped and unresourceful, except in the matter of charges, though you occasionally meet with ideal places. Therefore it is not advisable to delay too long making arrangements for putting up for the night—it is well to be in a position to go on easily to the next centre if there is no accommodation available in the spot first chosen.

It is often a difficult task to get meals in a lonely country district, except tea, which even cottagers will often cheerfully furnish. Hence it is a good plan to lay in and carry with you a fair stock of suitable provisions, and a thermos flask or two. You can then pursue your route in cheerful independence and enjoy a picnic meal in a picturesque spot.

SHROPSHIRE

The Welsh border counties, though exceptionally varied in scenic attractions, rich in historical associations, and dowered with many pleasant villages and townlets, are, it is safe to say, comparatively unknown even to the majority of English tourists. Though distant from London and the eastern side of England, they are very close to the Midland industrial centres, by which fortunately they are practically unaffected. Cheshire, the most northern of the three border counties, is outside our scope, as well as Monmouth in the south, which is really Welsh, but there is more than enough in Shropshire and Herefordshire.

There is an iron and coal working district round Wellington in Shropshire, but Newport, Market Drayton, Whitchurch and Wem are pleasant enough towns. Near Wellington is the old isolated 1,300 ft. hill of the Wrekin, with its forest recently sadly diminished, regarded by Salopians as the typical hill of the county, to which they accord the toast " to all round the Wrekin."

The geology of S. Shropshire is exceptionally varied; the Long Mynd is Cambrian, the varied shales and limestones of Ludlow belong to the Silurian system, and the district was the scene of the researches of Sir R. Murchison; Wenlock Edge contains much coral. Sandstone also occurs freely in the two counties; indeed Herefordshire is largely composed of Old Red Sandstone.

With regard to buildings, the Border counties have made an extensive use of their abundant oak woods, and half-timber houses may be found in nearly every district, ranging from cottages, or even dovecotes, as at Buttas and Luntley, to such a great Hall as Pitchford (Fig. 6). The timber work is not so elaborately patterned as in Cheshire, but is of a plainer panel type; both counties use limestone and the softer red sandstone.

There are not many outstanding churches in Shropshire. St. Mary's, Shrewsbury and Ludlow are very fine, veritable repositories of splendid craftsmanship in glass, and, at Ludlow, in wood. There are fine abbey or priory remains at Buildwas, Much Wenlock and Haughmond, north of

Shrewsbury. Church Stretton Church is interesting, and Oswestry, while Clun has the curious Welsh border belfry with a timber top; the latter two have timber lychgates. Bridgenorth has one old parish church, like Whitchurch, rebuilt in late Renaissance style. The Salopian churches have been the subject of a splendid monograph by the Very Rev. D. H. S. Cranage, now Dean of Norwich.

The border hills of Wales range across the outlying part of the north-west of the county, with the interesting old town of Oswestry on their edge; many Welsh names occur, and there are quarries and mines. It is not wise to rush through this stretch of country after the fashion of the "north and west" expresses, which take Shrewsbury to Hereford in an hour's stride. The real geological and communication centre of South Shropshire is at Craven Arms, at the end of Stretton Dale, where the ancient mass of the Long Mynd stretches to the west, with the Salop high road to Bishop's Castle rising twice to 1,200 feet, running between it and the parallel range of the Stiperstones, where mining for baryta and other minerals is carried on on a small scale. The Stretton Valley, with the three villages of Little Stretton, Church Stretton and All Stretton, has on its western side deep combe-like valleys cut by the streams from the Long Mynd. Among these is the Ashes Valley (Plate IV) and the Carding Mill Valley, with the cataract known as the "Light Spout." Across the Dale is the Caradoc Range of igneous origin, and showing a number of big whale-back hills, the Lawley, Ragleth, Hope Bowdler Hill, culminating in Caradoc's 1,650 feet, almost to a foot the exact height of the Long Mynd summit. The stretch of rolling country between these hills and Wenlock Edge is well worth a stay.

To the south-west of the county the huge bulge of the gaunt hills of Clun Forest projects into Wales, with the queer tiny town of Clun at its centre. The eight miles from Craven Arms Station to Clun up the valley of the Clun River are now spanned by a motor 'bus. From north to south Clun Forest is crossed by the road, roughly paralleled by the course of the early boundary, Offas Dyke, from

Radnorshire Knighton at its south edge on the Teme, through Clun to the quiet little market town of Bishop's Castle on a rise. Bishop's Castle is connected with Craven Arms by a funny little dead-end railway which retained its independence in the late amalgamation. Hopton Titterhill is a fine height with the ruined keep of Hopton Castle below it. The tourist should stroll up Bucknell Hill, 1,000 feet, and rejoice in one of the finest of the endless fair prospects with which Shropshire is favoured.

In the undulating wooded double range of Wenlock Edge are the fine old houses of Shipton Hall, Wilderhope, and thirteenth century Upper Millichope, with a shaft of its Early English window still carrying the hole for a defensive bar.

The River Teme is picturesque the whole way from its source at the Welsh end of Clun Forest till its merge in the Severn at Worcester. Nothing is more original or profitable than to follow its course, though the roads will mostly be broken, hilly byelanes, and good maps will be needed.

From the western side the shaggy heights of Wenlock Edge look down on the broad expanse of Corve Dale ; all is spaciously picturesque where the little Corve threads a succession of hamlets. West are the foot-hills of the great twin Clees, unique in England. The buttress-like foot-hills between Corve and Clee have winding, narrow, exceedingly hilly and picturesque lanes, which will give joy and possibly tribulation. This district ends north of Ludlow in a great boss of hills known as Hayton's Bent, underneath which is Stanton Lacy. From Ditton Priors a light railway has recently been constructed for the transport of the Clee Hill " Dhu " stone past Cleobury Mortimer, and thus bisects this isolated district.

The Severn, which has entered the county at the west, and meandered past Shrewsbury and industrial Coalbrookdale with Buildwas Abbey near, flows in a steep winding valley on the extreme east of the county. Finally, the Severn drifts into Worcestershire at the beautiful Forest of Wyre, in a district largely composed of cherry orchards.

Herefordshire can show larger and more settled villages; as with Shrewsbury, the county town of Hereford lies centrally, on the River Wye, the twin of the Severn, into whose estuary it finally falls. North-western Herefordshire is similar to Southern Shropshire. Its wooded hills look down on the Teme, and on the Lugg, which it is equally agreeable to explore from its Radnorshire source to its confluence with the Wye at Mordiford. In this district, with its Silurian hills, are the remains of a number of castles—Croft Castle, Richards Castle, etc.—a chain of border fortresses; at pretty Aymestrey the church still has a great beam to bar the door against marauders. Main rail and road run south from Ludlow to Hereford through Leominster, a place of many, if not broad, rivers and streams, where Lugg and Arrow and other brooks come together, not seldom in flood.

East of the Ludlow-Hereford road and rail stretches a fairly hilly pastoral district, sequestered and secluded, with many small hamlets connected by winding tangled lanes and offering many possibilities for exploration; Bromyard and picturesque Ledbury are the only towns of any size. The outline of the Worcestershire border is rambling and jagged, the Teme touches Herefordshire again for a small distance, and the Malvern Hills run for their whole ten-mile length on the eastern border, pierced by the railway and surmounted by the road from Worcester.

It is pleasant to follow up the course of the Wye westward from Hereford by a double road through country at first a little undulating and then hilly, till past Clifford Castle the little border town of Hay is reached, actually just outside the county limit where the river divides Radnorshire from Brecknock. Immediately to the south is the great mass of the Black Mountains, partly in Herefordshire, sloping down to the Golden Valley. It is not only pleasant to stroll through the Valley itself, but to ramble on each side by winding by-roads up the hills. But west is a fine field for touring over and between the first ridges of the Black Mountains round Longtown and Michaelchurch Eskley, by the early course of the Monnow.

South from Hereford the Wye swings in sinuous loops past Holme Lacy and Fawley to the little town of Ross, whence the wooded valley is famed for the beautiful vistas by Symonds Yat.

It will be seen, therefore, that Herefordshire can offer a typically pastoral type of wooded scenery, rising in the west to impressive heights. The county has never undergone industrial development, and consequently the villages are largely untouched, with many small hamlets. It is impossible to give detailed directions for the exploration of this sequestered county; Timmins' book is useful,* but the tourist can gain infinite pleasure by quartering a district with more or less improvised rambles. Dotted about are a few half-timber churches or belfries, always pleasurable. There is not a great number of churches of outstanding impressiveness, though Ross and Ledbury are of exceptional interest, but there is a curious little group of churches with detached belfries, fortress-like at Garway and of distinctive design, as mentioned already, at Pembridge and Yarpole.

Mention should be made of the Herefordshire architect, John Abell, who lived in Carolean times and lies buried under a stone with a curious inscription at Sarnesfield:

" This craggy stone a covering is for an architect's bed,
   That lofty buildings rais'd high, yet now lies low his head;
   His line and rule, so death concludes, are locked up in store:
   Build they who list or they who wist, for he can build no more.
   His house of clay will hold no longer,
   May heaven's joy build him a stronger."

The ignorant vandalism of later generations has dealt hardly with his timber market halls : the most elaborate at Hereford has disappeared and its aspect is now seen in earlier drawings. At Weobly the Hall has been wiped out, and at Leominster it was saved only by being re-erected as a private residence, " The Grange "; (Plate x) shows its original position. The hall remains at Ledbury, but one at Church Stretton has also been replaced by a neat structure of nineteenth century brick.

* *Nooks and Corners in Herefordshire.*

The upland Cotswolds consist entirely of oolitic limestone and often said to begin at Meon Hill, though of course the hills roll on into Northamptonshire. They form part of the great limestone belt which begins at the Dorset coast and sweeps north-west till it ends at the Humber. Over the Cotswold division the land slopes steadily upward from the Thames valley till it reaches 800-900 feet and (twice) 1,000 feet at the escarpment, overlooking the clay plains of the Avon and Severn. The Cotswold hills cover the major portion of Gloucestershire and all north Oxfordshire, taking in a tiny piece of Warwickshire and several peninsular and isolated scraps of Worcestershire scattered about. Oxford, as ever, is the Cotswolds' southern gate, knot of roads and rails from Banbury, Worcester, Cheltenham and other places, though from London to the North Cotswolds you may short circuit the university city. The first spot here described, Owlpen, lies in a tangled mass of wooded slopes near Nailsworth; hence by Stroud and Painswick the hills sweep round Cheltenham, which the projection of Cleeve's 1,070 feet separates from Winchcombe lying also in its cirque. Northward juts forth the outlier of Bredon Hill with two lesser outliers in between.

Cirencester, from which radiate the straight Roman roads, Fairford and Witney, lie on the Cotswold's southern edge. The Cotswold rivers all run down south or south-east to join the Thames in its westward course—by Cirencester is the Churn, the Coln threads its delightful villages down to Fairford, and the Windrush has a long course past Burford and Witney. The Oxford-Worcester railway is glad to follow the Evenlode's sinuous sweep, and the Banbury line takes the north-south valley of the Cherwell. Probably because of the frequent flooding of the narrow valley trenches no continuous road, except in the case of the Churn, follows the course of a river; the highways all keep the ridges, and consequently leave the villages comfortably and picturesquely tucked away beside the streams.

The buildings of the Cotswolds are indigenous and

distinctive ; the universal limestone has been applied to form a style as consistent as it is genuine and effective. The result is especially excellent when the building is roofed with the local Stonesfield slates, now unfortunately little quarried. One farmer reports that £1,000 was contributed by a Society to retain the original roofing of his splendid barn to avoid substituting corrugated iron. The old builders could make as excellent a job of a farmshed or a dovecote as of a stately church or a great manor house, but it is far cheaper now to build blatant red-brick, tiled roofed cottages than to employ the traditional masonry.

In addition to those described ante, there are delightful villages of all kinds, many, many of them ; churches which range from the smallest Norman building to the mighty late Perpendicular structures of wool-shearing prosperity—Campden, Winchcombe, Northleach, Cirencester ; barns, farmhouses, cottages, market halls, and country houses, chiefly Tudor, but also a respectable show of the later Renaissance. Explore for them, track them down, and revel in them !

THE CHALK HILLS

The Thames marks a distinct severance of character between the Berkshire Downs and the Chilterns. South of the river the edge of the hills runs roughly east to west, forming the northern limit of the great central chalk mass of Wiltshire. But from the Goring-Reading reach the Chilterns swing north-westward fairly parallel to the Cotswolds, sloping down S.E. from their 800 feet escarpment to the lower London clay. They occupy most of the Goring-Henley bend of the Thames, and continue as a well-defined belt of hill country, densely wooded with beech, and cut into valleys behind the main ridge. We leave them at the Buckinghamshire border, but the chalk hills go rolling on, first as the Dunstable Downs and then with ever-diminishing height through N. Herts into the east counties as well as upward into Lincs and Yorks. The whole way through Berks and Bucks the foot of the escarpment is dotted with a chain of villages of great character and charm ; even their names are pleasant-sounding—Kingston Lisle, Aston

Tirrold, Britwell Salome, Aston Rowant and many another. Many practicable roads run up over the hills in Berkshire, but after the edge with its prehistoric track the Downs are bare and lonely till you reach Lambourn in its valley, with a namesake river and a branch line, both running down to Newbury in the Kennet valley, which separates these hills by its sand-belt from the mightier chalk range which goes on into Hampshire. An almost unknown road keeps the Roman course from Speen by Newbury to Cirencester; it affords a romantic drive and connects two of our districts.

From the River you can run along the spine of the Chilterns by good roads to the northern Oxford Road, at 600-800 feet, an exhilarating experience. There are a fair number of upland villages and hamlets, mostly practising the curious indigenous craft of chair turning, but they are small settlements, with churches small or modern, or both. The two London-Oxford roads cross from Wycombe and Henley, north-westward, and the great dry valleys are utilised by main lines of rail. The Bucks-Oxon border wanders among the hills, but the natural division is found in the W. Wycombe-Princes Risborough cleft. Lastly let us look at the busy little town of Chesham, whose pretty little river Chess was a mighty stream in prehistoric times, fed by four great tributaries whose valleys are now dry.

THE EASTERN COUNTIES

See from the map how the three Eastern counties form a projection largely washed by the sea; it is not surprising that their geographical position has caused individual traits in their inhabitants and distinctiveness in their buildings.

All three counties are destitute of stone, which nevertheless has been used for some churches and greater houses by carriage by sea or by land from stone-bearing counties. Norfolk is well-known for its large use of brick, though Essex has made a greater use of brick in churches; its smaller churches are of southern county type, but often with interesting timber belfries. None of the three counties can lay claim to bold or hilly scenery, but they possess many charming undulating landscapes of a quiet pastoral type, and the series of meres connected by sluggish rivers, known as the Norfolk Broads, is individual, attractive, and not met with elsewhere.

ESSEX

Chelmsford, now the seat of a bishopric, is a pleasant town, while Colchester is of the highest interest for its Roman remains, churches and priory, and the fine Tudor interior at the Marquis of Granby Inn.

Smaller towns, like Braintree, Coggeshall, Witham, Kelvedon and Maldon are worthy of a visit, and there is a certain gaunt romance by some of the seaboard if care is taken to avoid the more recent watering-places. Mersea and Foulness Islands and the creeks are individual, and sometimes weird. Havering-atte-Bower is a jolly little place on a bold hill, known to many trained in the Artists' Rifles O.T.C. during the Great War. But the northern portion of the county will be found of particular interest; the Colne Valley through Halstead to Colchester is not terribly affected by its textile works.

In the chalk hill district around Saffron Walden and Thaxted, already described, such a village as Littlebury is an unfailing joy, and there is the surviving part of the great house at Audley End with its fine Tudor stables and alms-houses; while near Thaxted is the very vernacular example of Tudor brick at Horham Hall.

SUFFOLK

Suffolk like its neighbours is difficult to summarise; it possesses a vast number of villages in quiet surroundings. Indeed, the Norfolk diocese before its subdivision comprised over 900 churches, testifying to a once great country population.

No attempt is made to describe the coast watering-places, which it is usually unnecessary or inadvisable to visit, but Lowestoft has the fine Perpendicular flint church of St. Margaret, and Pakefield and Kessingland churches are also worth seeing. Blythburgh has a dignified and impressive church, a worthy companion to Southwold, while Wenhaston has one of the curious " doom " frescoes of the Middle Ages ; Aldeburgh too has its old Moot Hall. The only town of real commercial importance is Ipswich, which like most East Anglian places has surviving features of interest. Woodbridge, Beccles and Eye have fine churches, as also little Mildenhall in the Fens. To the southern edge of the county is the Stour Valley, known everywhere for its quiet scenery recorded by the brush of Constable (Plate XLVII). Clare, Cavendish and Glemsford are all delightful villages, with white plaster houses and stately churches, but lower down, leaving Long Melford and Sudbury for the moment, are Nayland and Stoke-by-Nayland, the latter on a bold knoll, where apart from the main street, a pair of Tudor timber houses make a fine group with the mighty church with its well-proportioned tall tower, largely built of brick. Sudbury has three churches, old houses, and associations with another painter, Thomas Gainsborough, though the hand of the destroyer has recently left its mark there. Long Melford can show a great church with a rebuilt tower, a large Hall, and many old houses and inns scattered about patches of green.

From Kersey (p. 112) it is only a step to Hadleigh, at the end of its little branch line, not to be confused with Hadleigh in Essex. Here the Deanery is one of the great tower-houses of Tudor brick, like Layer Marney in Essex and Oxburgh in Norfolk. There are many other pleasant houses and we can run on to Boxford, where the church has two equally fine porches, one stone and the other timber. To take one random instance, the little town of Framlingham has the remains of a castle, with a remarkably fine series of tombs in the church, and from there you can go on past Darsham and Yoxford, the " garden of Suffolk," to the great classic pile of Heveningham Hall, the seat of Lord Huntingfield. At Brandon, from pits which go back to prehistoric times, is carried on the most ancient craft in the world, for one or two expert flint knappers still make gun-flints for primitive tribes, and one inhabitant, though not a regular worker, has taught himself to chip flint arrowheads.

NORFOLK

Like its southern companion, Norfolk is a county of wide expanses with very many villages and old churches, but there are more small towns than in Suffolk, and practically all are of interest. Norwich and Great Yarmouth are the only towns of any commercial size. The former with its cathedral and castle has many quaint old houses and curious byways, which it is good to poke about; the scene on market days is crowded and animated. The view of the Cathedral from Pull's Ferry is impressive and at Heigham, a mile away, the flint Dolphin Inn was once the Bishop's Palace. Yarmouth, though a seaside resort, is still an old fishing town, and it is worth glancing at its wide-aisled church of St. Nicholas, St. George's Fisherman's Hospital, and the queer narrow " Rows." Small towns are : Downham Market, Swaffham, Thetford, Stoke Ferry, Watton, Diss, Harleston, Aylsham, North Walsham, Fakenham, Holt, East Harling with its fine tower and leaden spirelet. West from Norwich, Wymondham was once famed for the manufacture of taps and spigots, which are carved on the octagonal little timber market house.

To those who find an attraction in old churches, Norfolk offers unending possibilities, from tiny hamlet buildings to great cathedral-like piles. We can think, for instance, of the great church of Sall, Necton near Swaffham, with its glorious roof, the huge flint tower of Deopham and many another. The Perpendicular style of the fifteenth century occurs almost universally through Norfolk, witnessing the prosperity of the county at the end of the Middle Ages. Most of the churches are in flint—often elaborately panelled, as at St. Peter Mancroft, Norwich—glorious with carved roofs of single or double hammer-beams, with rows of angels with outstretched wings. In addition there are many screens, stalls and other mediaeval craftsmanship. The discerning tourist who knows how to ramble will make discoveries—such a church as Beeston, for instance, practically unknown, cannot fail to be a joy. Norfolk is the county of round towers, a form suited to flint and dispensing with stone. Many of these towers were originally Saxon or Norman, of which period much work remains on south doors. Occasionally round towers have been completed by octagonal lanterns. Some smaller Norman churches retain the apse, and in a number of cases the thatched roof still survives, as at Hailes and Edingthorpe. The meres or Broads provide in their reeds the finest thatching material.

Rivers form nearly the whole southern boundary of the county—by Wisbech on the Fen lands to the east we have the old River Nen. The Little Ouse runs north-east through Hilgay Fen, and joins the Ouse past King's Lynn to the sea; it is earlier known as the Brandon River. The Waveney also parts the county from Suffolk until it joins the Yare from Norwich at Breydon Water, near Yarmouth. Between Swaffham and Thetford is the individual lonely heath country, sparsely inhabited, with slightly undulating sandhills and scattered clumps of pine. Among it is the great pile of Oxburgh and the Tudor house of Great Cressingham, with a towered hall also at Fincham.

In the top part of the county, north from King's Lynn, bounded by the Wash, is the royal residence at Sandringham, the fine spired Decorated church at Snettisham, and the collection of Burnham villages, of which Burnham Thorpe has the Rectory where Nelson was born. There is an old house at Stiffkey, and great eighteenth century piles have been built in parks near by, at Holkham and Houghton. Wolterton, a smaller solid contemporary structure, is north of Aylsham. There is also the fine Early Renaissance seat at Blickling, with Felbrigg Hall near Cromer. The late seventeenth century house of Melton Constable has beautiful modelled plasterwork.

The individual Broad country is in a triangle, of which the line Norwich-Yarmouth is the base and North Walsham the apex, the eastern side being bounded by the sea. The Broads can only be explored satisfactorily by water, and a Broadland holiday on a wherry or motorboat has many attractions. The shallow reedy meres are accessible by the sluggish Bure from Wroxham to Yarmouth, and its tributaries the Ant and Thurne. It is curious that the ends of these dyke-like rivers are occasionally but a mile or two from the sea, from the incursion of which the land is only protected by a line of sand dunes ; thus from Horsey Mere it is possible to enjoy a sea bathe. In the Broadland country the group of churches with painted screens is worth exploring ; Ranworth is the most famous, but Ludham and Irstead are also remarkable.

It is unnecessary to discuss the modern seaside places, but there are pleasant little coast villages, as at Happisburgh, and Mundesley gives access to the fine font-cover of Trunch, as well as Knapton roof (Plate XLIV).

Fig. 28.——Hedingham Castle.

Drawn by Sydney Newcombe.

INDEX

TO TEXT AND ILLUSTRATIONS

(The figures in heavy type denote illustrations in text.)

Abbey Dore, 48, 49, Church, Pl. xi
Abdon, 17
Abingdon, 67, 68, Christ's Hospital, 69;
    Church, Pl. xxii
Ablington, 57
Acton Burnell, 34, 35
Aldbury, 85
Aldeburgh, 125
Aldsworth, 57
All Stretton, 15
Almshouses, Chipping Campden, Pl. xxi
Amersham, 82, 83, Inn, Pl. xxxi
Anna Regina, 56
Ape Dale, 12, 13, 15
Arnold, Matthew, quoted, 68
Arrow, River, 43, 46, Pl. ix
Ash Valley, Pl. iv
Aston-on-Clun, 31
Aston Subedge, 62
Aston Tirrold, 72
Attleborough, 101
Aymestrey, 41, 42, 43

Barnham Broom, 104
Barns, ancient, at High Roding, Pl. xxxv;
    at Moulsford, Pl. xxvii
Barrett, C. R. B., *Essex Highways*, etc., 89
Barrow, 11
Baxter, Richard, 6
Beaconsfield, 82
Beckett, R., *Romantic Essex*, 89
Bell-cote, wooden, 50, Pl. xi
Belloc, Hilaire, on Abingdon, 67
Berkeley Vale, 55
Berkshire Downs, 122-123, Map III
Bettws y Crwyn, 33
Bibury, 56, 57, Pl. xvi
Bircher, 41
Bishops Castle, 33, 118
Blakeney, interior of Church, Pl. xii;
    Church, with lighthouse, Pl. xliii
Bledlow, 79
Blewbury, 72
Boscobel House, 38, 39, portrait of Dame
    Alice Penderel, 38
Bourton-on-the-Water, 58, Pl. xviii
Bradenham, 84
Bradwell, ruins near, 90
Brampton Bryan, 30
Brandon, Pl. xli
Bravinium, 29

Brecon Beacons, 41
Bridgenorth, 5, 6, 7, 117, Pl. ii; St. Mary's
    Steps, Pl. ii; Rock House, Pl. ii
Brill, 83, 85, 86, Pl. xxxii
Bringewood Chase, 19
Broads, The, 110, 127, Pl. xxxiii; Fritton
    Church, Pl. xlv
Broadway, 63
Broadway Hill, 61
Bromfield, 28, Pl. vi
Brooke, Rupert, 85
Broseley, 11
Brown Clee, 27
Brown Clee Hill, 16
Buckinghamshire, North, and the Chil-
    terns, 65 ff., 122-123; old Lace-Maker,
    Pl. xxiii
Buckland, 63
Bucknell, 30, view from South, Pl. vi
Burford, 57, Pl. xvii
Burke, Edmund, 79, 83
Burney, Dr. Charles, 38
Burnham Beeches, 79, Pl. xxx
Bury Saint Edmonds, 99, St. James's
    Church, Pl. xxxix; "Dog and Par-
    tridge," Pl. xl
By-Lanes, Exploring, 3, 53, 86, 90, 98,
    110, 112, 123

Caer Caradoc, 12
Capstone Mill, 77
Carding Mill Valley, 14
Carr, Rev. Donald, 14
Castle Hedingham, 112, 113, 128
Chair-making, 77, 79
Chalfont Saint Giles, 81, Milton's Cottage,
    Pl. xxxi
Chalfont Saint Peter, 81
Chapman, John, strange story of, 105
Chaucer, family associations, 75, 76
Cheltenham, 53
Chenies, 83
Childrey, 69
Chinnor, 79
Chipping Campden, 60, 61, 62, Alms-
    houses, Pl. xxi; Church and river, Pl.
    xxi; Sheep Market, Pl. xx; Wool Fair,
    Pl. xx
Church Stretton, 14, 15
Cirencester, 56
Clare, 97, 98, Pl. xxxviii

129

INDEX

Clee Hills, 17, 27, 41
Clee St. Margaret's, 18
Cleobury Mortimer, 26
Cley, 109
Clifton Hampden, Inn, **67**
Clun, 31, 32
Clunbury, 31
Clungunford, 31
Cobbett, William, on Herefordshire, 18
Coggeshall, 90
Coleswell Mill, 56, Pl. xvi
Coln, River, 56
Coln Saint Denis, 57, 58
Condover Hall, 36, Pl. vii
Constable, John, 125, Water Lane, Stratford, Suffolk, Pl. xlvii
Cookley Green, 75
Corve Dale, 16, Chapel, **16**, Pl. iv
Cotswolds, The, 53 ff., 121-122, Map II
Coxwell Knoll, 30
Craik, Mrs., *John Halifax, Gentleman*, 64
Craven Arms, 33
Cricklade, 56
Croft Ambrey, 41
Cuddington, 86
Cutsdean, 58

Darwin, Charles, 38
Dashwood Hill, 78
Deerfold Forest, 43
Defoe, Daniel, on Bury Saint Edmonds, 99
Denver, Mill at, Pl. xxxiii
Deopham Church, 104
Diddlebury, or Delbury, 15
D'Israeli, Benjamin, 79, 84
Ditton Priors, 17
Dorchester-on-Thame, 65, 66
Dorstone, 51, Arthur's Stone, Pl. xi
Dovecotes, Buttas, 116, Eardisland, Pl. ix ; Luntley, 44, 116 ; Much Marcle, **47**
Dover's Hill, 62
Downton on the Rock, 29
"Ducking," Pl. xxiii ; ducking stool at Leominster, 46, **48**

Eardisland, 43, dovecote, Pl. ix
East Dereham, 108
East Hagbourne, 72, Pl. xxvi
East Harling, 101
Eastern Counties, 87 ff.
Ellwood, Thomas, 81
Elton, 39
Essex, 89 ff., 113, 124, Map V
Evesham, Vale of, 63
Ewelme, 75, 76

Fairford, 56
Faringdon, 69
Fens, The, 88, 107, 127, Pl. xxxiv
Finchingfield, 91, 92, Village Green, Pl. xxxvi

Fingest, 78, Church, Pl. xxix
Fosse Way, the, 57, 60
Fritton, 110, Church, Pl. xlv
Froude, J. A., 83
Fyfield Manor House, 68, Pl. xxv

Gainsborough, Thomas, 112
Garboldisham Heath, 101
Gasthorpe, 100
Golden Valley, the, 47 ff.
Goodrich Castle, 51, 52, Pl. xii
Gray, Thomas, 79
Great Cressingham, 106
Great Hampden, 85

Hadleigh (Suffolk), 125
Hampden, John, 79, 88
Hampton Court (Herefordshire), 47
Hardingham, 104
Hartest, 98, Pl. xxxviii
Hartswood, scenery at, Pl. xxvii
Harwell, 72
Hawkeden, 98
Hay, 51
Heath, The Chapel on, 16, 48
Hedingham Castle, 112, 113, **128**
Hempstead, 89, 97
Herefordshire, 42 ff., 119-120, Map I
High Roding, 90, barn at, xxxv
High Wycombe, 79
Hingham, 103, 104
Holgate, William, 96
Hopton Cangeford, 18, 19
Hopton Castle, 30
Housman, A. E., *Shropshire Lad*, quoted, 12
Hughenden, 84
Hughes, Thomas, 69
Hunstanton, 108, Pl. xliii

Icknield Way, The, 75, 77
Inns, Lodgings and Meals, 115 ; Amersham, Pl. xxxi ; Bibury, 56, Pl. xvi ; Bourton-on-the-Hill, 64 ; Bury Saint Edmonds, 99, Pl. xxxix ; Clifton Hampden, **67** ; Clun, 31 ; Finchingfield, 92 ; Fingest, 78 ; Hempstead, 89 ; Hingham, 103 ; King's Lynn, 104, 106 ; Langley, 81, 82 ; Lavenham, 111 ; Ludlow, 21 ; Munslow, 15, 16 ; North Walsham, 104 ; Paradise, 53 ; Saffron Walden, 96 ; Stoke Row, 77 ; Tewkesbury, 64
Ivinghoe, 85

Jeffreys, Judge, 38
Jones, Sydney R., Wilderhope, **13** ; Cottage topiary, **40** ; Market House, Pembridge, 44 ; View of Church, Weobley, **45** ; School Porch, Weobley, **46** ; Ducking Stool, Leominster, **48** ; Owlpen Manor House, Entrance, 54 ; Yews,

INDEX

55; Pargetted house at Steventon, **74**; Parham Old Hall, **91**; Customs House, King's Lynn, **107**
Jordans, 80, 81, Meeting House, Pl. xxx

Kelvedon, 90
Kempsford, 56, Pl. xvi
Kerry Pole, 33
Kersey, 112, Pl. xlvi
Kilpeck, 48, Church, **49**
King's Lynn, 106, 107, Customs House, **107**; Old Market, Pl. xlii
Knapton, 109, Church nave roof, Pl. xliv
Knighton, 33

Lace maker, Pl. xxiii
Laindon, 91
Lambourn, 70
Langham, the Mill, Pl. xxxv
Langland, William, *Vision of Piers Plowman*, 27
Langley, 35, 36, 81
Lavenham, 111, 112, Church Street, 111, Lady Street, Pl. xlv
Lechdale, 56
Ledbury, 51, 52, 120, Market Street, 51, Houses, Pl. xiv
Lee, Lee, Richard, 34
Lee, Colonel Richard, 36
Leinthall Earls, 41
Leintwardine, 29
Leland, John, *Itinerary* quoted, on Ludlow, 19, 20; Cleobury Mortimer, 26; Clee Hills, 27; Stokesay, 34; Shrewsbury, 36, 37; Abbey Dore, 49; Kingston Bagpuze, 68; Bury Saint Edmonds, 99, 100
Leominster, 46, 47, Ducking Stool, 48, Market Hall, Pl. x
Lighthouse, mediaeval, Pl. xliii
Little Dunmow, 92, 93
Little Stretton, 15
Lodgings and Meals, 114-115
Long Crendon, 83
Long Leinthall, 39
Long Mynd, 14, entrance to the Ash Valley, Pl. iv
Lower Brockhampton Hall, Pl. xiii
Lower Slaughter, 58, 59, Pl. xviii
Ludford Bridge, 19, 25
Ludgershall, Lace-maker of, Pl. xxiii
Ludlow, 19, 20, 21; Broad Street, Pl. v; Castle, 23, 23, 24, Pl. v; Reader's House, **21**
Lugg, River, 46, 47

Maldon, 90
Malvern Hills, 41
Mapledurham, old Mill, Pl. xxviii
Market Drayton, 8, *Frontispiece*

Mary Knowl, 39
Masefield, John, quoted, 2
Mayflower, The, 81
Mickleton, 62
Mills, at Coleswell, 56, Pl. xvi; Denver, Pl. xxiii; East Anglian, Pl. xxxiii; Pl. xxxv; Langham, Pl. xxxv; Mapledurham, Pl. xxviii; Streatley-on-Thames, xxviii
Milton, John, 78, 81, his Cottage, Pl. xxxi
Moats, Oxburgh, xli; Parham, **91**
Monks Risborough, 85
Morley St. Botolph, 104
Morville, 8
Moulsford, thatched barn, Pl. xxvii
Much Marcle, dovecote, 44, **47**
Much Wenlock, 9, 10, Stocks at, **9**, Ruins, **11**
Munslow, 15

Nailsworth, 54
Necton, 104
Newbury, 70, 71, Bridge, Pl. xxvi
Newcastle, 33
Newcombe, Sydney, Hedingham Castle, **128**
Newport, 8
Nordy Bank, Roman camp, 16
Norfolk, 87 ff., 126-128; River scenery, Pl. xxxiv; Water-mills, Pl. xxxv, Map V
Northleach, 57, 58, Church porch, Pl. xvii
Norwich, 126

Ombersley, 2
Onny, River, 28
Orleton, 41
Ouse, the, at Brandon, Pl. xli
Owlpen, 54, 121, Manor House, **54**, clipped Yews, **55**
Oxburgh, 106, Hall and Moat, Pl. xli
Oxfordshire, 53 ff., 121-122, Map II

Painswick, 53, Church, Pl. xiv
Pant Valley, 91
Paradise, 53
Pargetting, examples of, 73, **74**, 92
Parham Old Hall, 90, **91**
Parr, Thomas, 39
Paston, its associations, 110
Pembridge, 43, Market House, **44**, Church, Pl. x
Penderel, Dame Alice, portrait, **38**
Penn, village, 83
Penn, William, 79, 80, 81, 82
Percy, Thomas, 6
Peterchurch, 50, 51
Pipe Aston, 39
Pitchford Hall, **35**, 36
Pontrilas, 48
Poslingford, 98
Princes Risborough, 76, 78, Pl. xxxii

INDEX

Quatford, 3
Quatt, 3, 4

Radnor Forest, 30
Ragleth Hill, 12
Ranworth, 110, 128, Church screen, Pl. xliv
Richard's Castle, 39, 41
Roding, River, 90
Ross-on-Wye, 52, 120, Pl. xii, Market House, Pl. xiii
Rubens, Sir P. P., 81

Saffron Walden, 96, 97, Pl. xxxvii
Saint Devereux, 48
Saint Margaret's, 50, Pl. xi
Salthouse Heath, 109
Sapperton, 56, Pl. xv
Scole, 101, "White Hart," 101
Scoulton, 104
Scott, Sir Walter, 86
Severn Gorge, the, 4
Shipdham, 108
Shrewsbury, 7, 36, 37, 38, Old Grammar School, Pl. viii
Shropshire, 2 ff., 116-118, Map I
Sible Hedingham, 113
Sinodun Hill, Pl. xxiv
Southwold, 110
Sparsholt, 69
Stanton, 63, Warren House, Pl. xxii
Stanton Lacy, 28
Stanway, 63
Steeple Bumpstead, 97
Steventon, 73, house, 74
Stiffkey, 109
Stocks, old, Perigrinating, 9
Stoke Prior, Pl. viii
Stoke Ross, 77
Stokesay Castle, 33, 34, Pl. vii
Stow, John, quoted, 93
Stowlangtoft, 100
Stow-on-the-Wold, 57, 59, 60
Stratford (Suffolk), Water Lane, Pl. xlvii
Streatley, old Mill, Pl. xxviii
Stretton, 41
Stretton Dale, 15
Stretton Sugwas, cottage, 40
Sudbury, 112, Pl. xlvii
Suffolk, 97 ff., 124-125, Map V
Swaffham, 105, 106
Swift, Jonathan, 52
Swinbrook, 58
Swyncombe, 77
Symond's Yat, 120

Teme, River, 19, 118
Tewkesbury, 64
Thames Valley, scenery, Pl. xxvi, Pl. xxvii, Pl. xxviii

Thaxted, 94, Pl. xxxvi, Moot Hall, Pl. xxxvii
Thetford, 106
Thompson, Peddar's Way, Pl. xl
Thorpe Market, 109
Throckmorton, Sir John, 68, 70
Thurston End, 98
Titterstone Clee 17, 27
Topiary, examples of, 8, 40, 55
Travellers, hints for, 114-115
Turnastone, 50
Turpin, Dick, 89
Turville Heath, 77

Uffington, 69
Upper Slaughter, 58, 59, Pl. xix
Upper Swell, 59, the Manor, Pl. xix
Upper Winchenden, 86
Uriconium, 36

Vale Royal, 17
Vaux, Rev. J. E., quoted, 95
Vowchurch, 50

Wales, borders of, 8 ff.
Waller, Edmund, 79
Wallingford, 73, scenery near, Pl. xxvii
Walpole, Horace, 84
Walsham-le-Willow, 100
Wantage, 72
Ward, Mrs. Humphry, 85
Watling Street, 15
Wem, 8
Wenlock Edge, view from, 12, Pl. iii
Weobley, 43, 44, street in, 45, school porch, 46
West Wycombe, 78, 79, Pl. xxix
Westington Hill, 61
Whitchurch, 7, 8
Whitcliff, 25, 26
White Horse Hill, 69, 70, Pl. xxv
Whittington Castle, Pl. iii
Wiggenhall St. German's, Pl. xlii
Wigmore, 39, 41, Gatehouse, 42, 43, Pl. ix
Wilderhope, 13
Willersey, 63
Willingdales, the, 90
Winchcombe, 64
Windrush, River, 58
Witham (Essex), 90
Wittenham Clumps, 66, 67, Pl. xxiv
Woburn Abbey, 84
Wormsley Valley, 77
Wrekin, The, 12, 36
Wroxeter, 36
Wye Valley, 51, 52
Wymondham, 101, Church, 102

Yare, River, Pl. xxiv
Yarmouth, Great, 126
Yarpole, 43

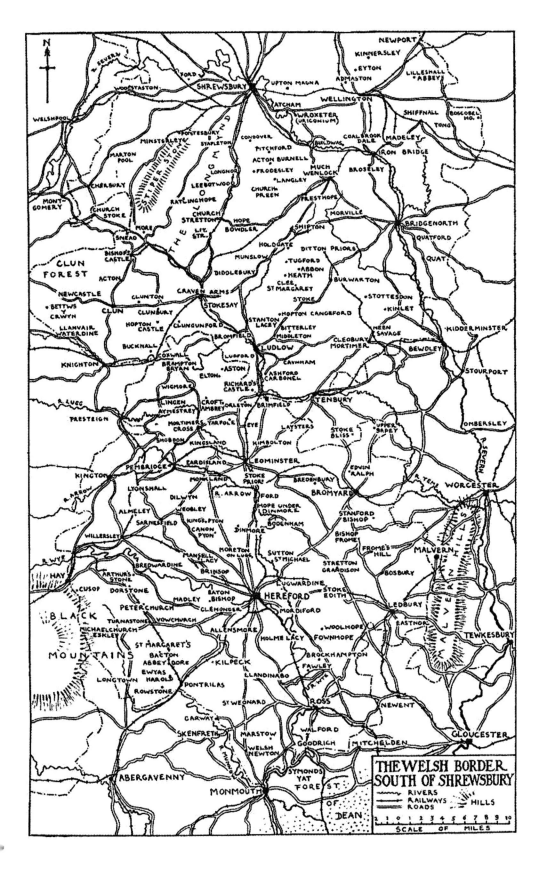

THE WELSH BORDER
SOUTH OF SHREWSBURY

RIVERS
RAILWAYS
ROADS
HILLS

SCALE OF MILES

THE
COTSWOLDS

RIVERS
RAILWAYS
ROADS   HILLS
COUNTY BOUNDARIES

1 0 1 2 3 4 5 6   12
SCALE OF MILES

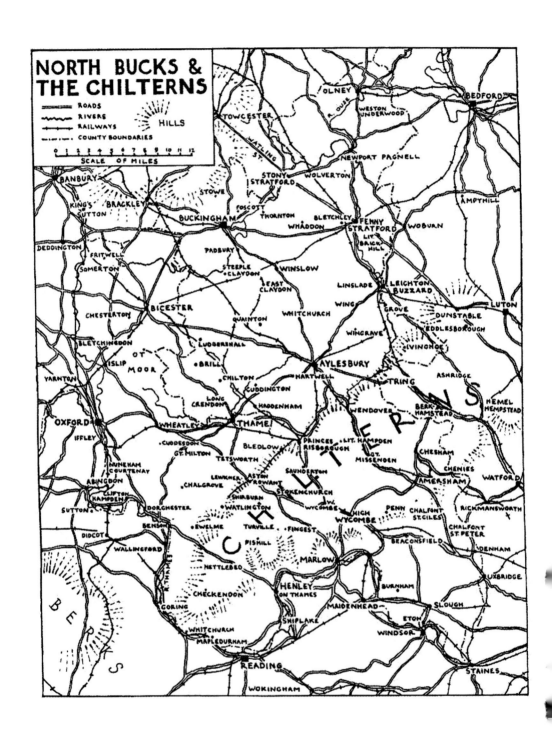

NORTH BUCKS &
THE CHILTERNS

ROADS
RIVERS
RAILWAYS
COUNTY BOUNDARIES
HILLS

0 1 2 3 4 5 6 7 8 9 10 11 12
SCALE OF MILES

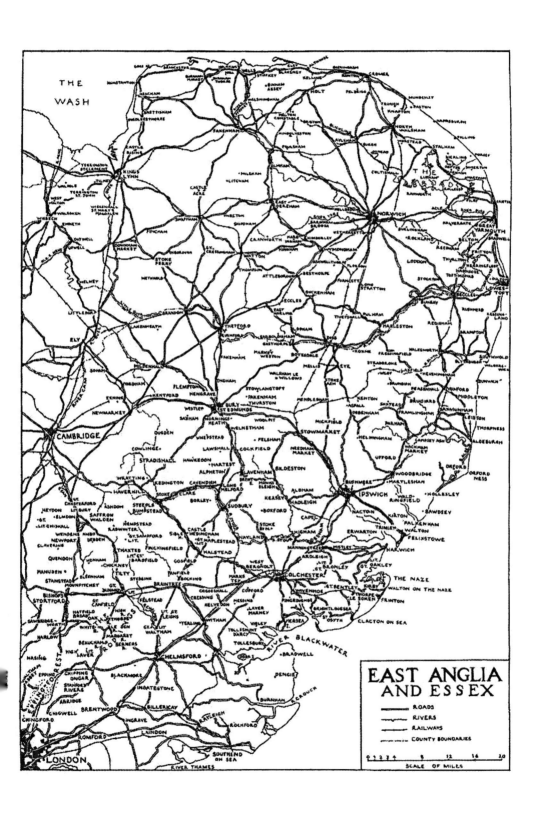

EAST ANGLIA
AND ESSEX

————	ROADS	
˄˄˄˄	RIVERS	
⊢⊢⊢⊢	RAILWAYS	
·−·−·−	COUNTY BOUNDARIES	

0 1 2 3 4   8   12   16   20

SCALE OF MILES

Printed in the United Kingdom
by Lightning Source UK Ltd.
123108UK00001B/4/A

9 781905 217793